brilliant

Microsoft®
Outlook
2007

POCKET BOOK

Meryl K. Evans

PEARSON

Prentice
Hall

Harlow, England • London • New York • Boston • San Francisco • Toronto
Sydney • Tokyo • Singapore • Hong Kong • Seoul • Taipei • New Delhi
Cape Town • Madrid • Mexico City • Amsterdam • Munich • Paris • Milan

Pearson Education Limited
Edinburgh Gate
Harlow CM20 2JE
Tel: +44 (0)1279 623623
Fax: +44 (0)1279 431059
Website: www.pearsoned.co.uk

First published in Great Britain in 2007

@ Joli Ballew 2007

The right of Meryl K. Evans to be identified as author of this work has been asserted by her in accordance with the Copyright, Designs and Patents Act 1988.

ISBN: 978-0-132-05971-8

British Library Cataloguing-in-Publication Data
A catalogue record for this book is available from the British Library

Microsoft product screen shots reprinted with permission from Microsoft Corporation.

10 9 8 7 6 5 4 3 2 1
11 10 09 08 07

Typeset in 10pt Helvetica by 3
Printed and bound in Great Britain by Ashford Colour Press Ltd., Gosport

The Publisher's policy is to use paper manufactured from sustainable forests.

Brilliant Pocket Books

What you need to know – when you need it!

When you're working on your PC and come up against a problem that you're unsure how to solve, or want to accomplish something in an application that you aren't sure how to do, where do you look? If you are fed up with wading through pages of background information in unwieldy manuals and training guides trying to find the piece of information or advice that you need RIGHT NOW, and if you find that helplines really aren't that helpful, then Brilliant Pocket Books are the answer!

Brilliant Pocket Books have been developed to allow you to find the info that you need easily and without fuss and to guide you through each task using a highly visual step-by-step approach – providing exactly what you need to know, when you need it!

Brilliant Pocket Books are concise, easy-to-access guides to all of the most common, important and useful tasks in all of the applications in the Office 2007 suite. Short, concise lessons make it really easy to learn any particular feature, or master any task or problem that you will come across in day-to-day use of the applications.

When you are faced with any task on your PC, whether major or minor, that you are unsure about, your Brilliant Pocket Book will provide you with the answer – almost before you know what the question is!

Brilliant Pocket Books Series

Series Editor: Joli Ballew

Brilliant Microsoft® Access 2007 Pocket Book	*S.E. Slack*
Brilliant Microsoft® Excel 2007 Pocket Book	*J. Peter Bruzzese*
Brilliant Microsoft® Office 2007 Pocket Book	*Jerri Ledford & Rebecca Freshour*
Brilliant Microsoft® Outlook 2007 Pocket Book	*Meryl K. Evans*
Brilliant Microsoft® PowerPoint 2007 Pocket Book	*S.E. Slack*
Brilliant Microsoft® Windows Vista Pocket Book	*Jerri Ledford & Rebecca Freshour*
Brilliant Microsoft® Word 2007 Pocket Book	*Deanna Reynolds*

Contents

Introduction

Welcome to the *Brilliant Microsoft® Outlook 2007 Pocket Book* – a handy visual quick reference that will give you a basic grounding in the common features and tasks that you will need to master to use Microsoft® Outlook 2007 in any day-to-day situation. Keep it on your desk, in your briefcase or bag – or even in your pocket! – and you will always have the answer to hand for any problem or task that you come across.

Find out what you need to know – when you need it!

You don't have to read this book in any particular order. It is designed so that you can jump in, get the information you need and jump out – just look up the task in the contents list, turn to the right page, read the introduction, follow the step-by-step instructions – and you're done!

How this book works

Each section in this book includes foolproof step-by-step instructions for performing specific tasks, using screenshots to illustrate each step. Additional information is included to help increase your understanding and develop your skills – these are identified by the following icons:

 Jargon buster – New or unfamiliar terms are defined and explained in plain English to help you as you work through a section.

 Timesaver tip – These tips give you ideas that cut corners and confusion. They also give you additional information related to the topic that you are currently learning. Use them to expand your knowledge of a particular feature or concept.

 Important – This identifies areas where new users often run into trouble, and offers practical hints and solutions to these problems.

Brilliant Pocket Books are a handy, accessible resource that you will find yourself turning to time and time again when you are faced with a problem or an unfamiliar task and need an answer at your fingertips – or in your pocket!

1

Getting Started with Outlook 2007

In this lesson you'll learn about the new features that Outlook 2007 provides and learn how to open Outlook in both Windows XP and Vista.

The first release of Outlook came bundled with Exchange Server 5.5 in 1997 with a primary role as an e-mail application. In its ten years, Outlook grew from an e-mail application to a personal information manager. Microsoft added a calendar, contacts and tasks into later editions, but each application behaved more as an individual entity than as part of a whole. Outlook 2007 changed that with its tight and seamless integration of mail, calendar, contacts and tasks. In addition to its predecessors' basic functions of sending and receiving e-mails, managing appointments and creating tasks, Outlook 2007 comes with the following new features:

- **Instant search**: Search information in e-mails, calendars, tasks, contacts and notes by keywords, date and other criteria.

- **To-Do bar**: Get an overview of your day in one place, including due tasks, flagged e-mail and upcoming appointments.

- **Colour categories**: Assign colour categories to information for easier organisation and searching.

- **Flag e-mails as tasks**: Flag e-mails as tasks for a quick way to create new tasks from e-mails in one step.

- **Preview attachments**: Get a quick glance of the attachment in the reading pane without opening the file.

- **Calendar sharing**: Share calendars with others inside and outside of your organisation.

- **Calendar view**: View multiple calendars side by side in one view.

- **Text messaging**: Send text messages from within e-mail.

- **RSS feeds**: Read RSS feeds in your inbox.

■ **Electronic business cards**: Customise and share electronic business cards.

The biggest difference is the ability to read and write e-mails, manage appointments, check tasks and find contacts all within one window. Outlook also makes it easier to find information with its new integration capabilities. Rather than finding tasks within tasks, and creating new tasks from scratch based on an e-mail, you can flag an e-mail as a new task in one step and see tasks in the calendar based on their due dates. Outlook 2007 adds many new features and a redesigned interface to qualify this as a major upgrade from earlier versions to become a complete information manager.

→ How to Use this Book

If you're eager to get going with all the basic features, Chapter 2 quickly touches on all the major aspects of Outlook. When you're ready to dig deeper into a feature, jump to the related chapter.

Figure 1.1
Reviewing Outlook's modules.

Since the goal of this book is to give you what you need when you need it, the book highlights the regularly used features and provides hints along the way for continued exploration beyond the book.

Outlook consists of Calendar, Contacts, Mail, Tasks and other components, as Figure 1.1 shows. This book refers to them as folders and modules.

→ Special Note about Vista and Windows XP

In this book, the graphics and some instructions, especially those related to the operating system, reflect the Vista interface. However, you can use this book with Windows XP or Vista. Windows XP and Vista differ mainly in appearance rather than functionality. For example, the folder icons appear in 3D in Vista instead of as a flat image in Windows XP. The **Start** button appears round with a Windows icon in Vista, like the one shown in Figure 1.2, and rectangular with the word 'Start' in Windows XP, as Figure 1.3 shows.

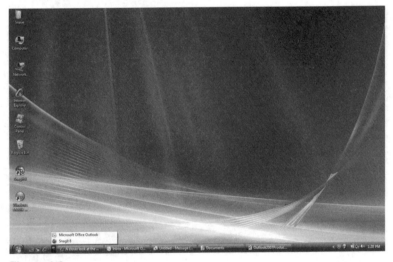

Figure 1.2
The Start button in Vista.

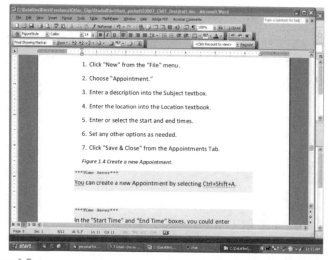

Figure 1.3

The Start button in Windows XP.

To open Outlook in Windows XP, follow these steps:

1 Click **Start**.

2 Click **All Programs**.

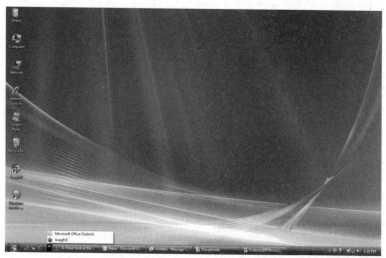

Figure 1.4

Access Outlook from the Quick Launch menu in Vista.

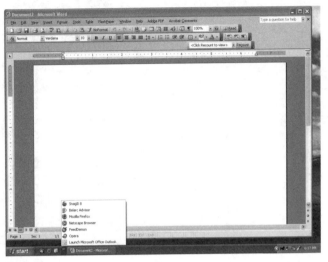

Figure 1.5
Access Outlook from the Quick Launch menu in Windows XP.

3 Select **Microsoft Office**.

4 Choose **Microsoft Office Outlook 2007**.

You may be able to access Outlook from the Quick Launch menu next to the Start button similar to the one shown in Vista in Figure 1.4. If you don't see the Outlook icon, click **>>** and it should appear in the menu that opens, as Figure 1.5 shows.

→ Doing Tasks

Outlook, as with other Microsoft products and software, has multiple ways to accomplish a task. This book uses the most common and simplest steps in showing how to do each task. You're welcome to do the steps in a different way. Please feel free to experiment with other ways and find what works best for you. This book aims to show you, with help from pictures, how to do many tasks with Outlook 2007. The purpose is to help you do what you need in the fewest steps, and to pick up a few new tricks that eventually you can't imagine working without.

Timesaver tip

You can quickly access many features in Outlook by right-clicking an item or space to open a menu.

2

Getting Started Quickly with Outlook 2007

In this lesson you'll learn how to start and close Outlook and become familiar with the new Ribbon feature and Outlook 2007 Interface. There are also quick introductions to reading, creating, replying to and forwarding e-mails as well as adding appointments, contacts, journal entries, notes and tasks.

→ Starting Outlook

This chapter digs right into Outlook and shows you how to do most of its basic and more frequently used features. The later chapters cover these in more detail. Ready to meet Outlook 2007? Open Outlook by taking the following steps:

1 Click the **Start** button.

2 Select **Programs**.

3 Click **Microsoft Office**.

4 Choose **Microsoft Office Outlook 2007**.

Figure 2.1 shows how to open Outlook using the Start button.

Before you write your first e-mail message in Outlook 2007, meet the Ribbon.

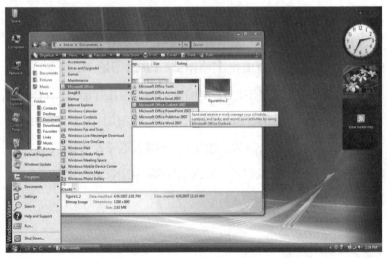

Figure 2.1
Open Outlook 2007.

Timesaver tip

You can quickly access Journal by adding the Journal view button to the Navigation Pane. Click the down arrow at the bottom of the left-hand sidebar, choose **Add or Remove Buttons** and click **Journal**.

→ Closing Outlook

When you finish working with Outlook for the session, you can close it. However, if you have a new e-mail message and you try to close Outlook without saving or sending the message, Outlook lets you know there is an unsent message and asks whether you want to exit without sending or not exit. If you choose **Exit Without Sending**, then it asks whether you want to save changes. This also applies to any unsaved calendar, tasks and other open items.

To close Outlook, do the following steps:

1 Click the **X** located at the top right-hand corner of Outlook's window.

2 If you've saved all documents, Outlook closes. If not, Outlook asks whether you want to save the changes.

You can also click the **X** in any open window within Outlook, including open e-mails, events, tasks and notes. Another way to close **Outlook** is to click the Outlook button in the upper left-hand corner of Outlook and click **Close**, or double-click the **Outlook** button.

Managing E-mail

In this lesson you'll learn how to create an e-mail account, create messages and personalise them with signatures, themes and stationery. You'll also learn how to work with e-mail attachments.

→ Creating an E-mail Account

The simplifying of creating a new e-mail account with the wizard, is one of the more notable improvements in Outlook 2007. Who wants to enter more than an e-mail address and password to set up an account? Some Internet service providers don't make it easy to access the needed e-mail account configuration information. Outlook 2007 takes that part off your hands with its wizard.

The wizard, however, doesn't always work. If this is the case for you, you'll need to set up the e-mail account manually.

Creating an E-mail Account with Auto Account Setup

Just do the following steps and Outlook should take care of the rest (this does not apply to Exchange accounts):

1   Select **Account Settings** from the Tools menu.

2   Click **New**, as shown in Figure 3.1.

Figure 3.1

Account Settings window for managing accounts.

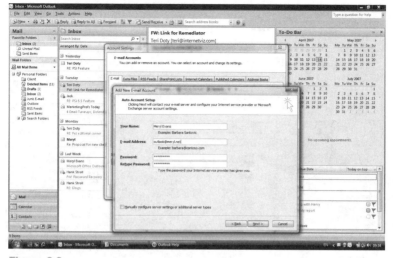

Figure 3.2
Auto Account Setup simplifies creating a new account.

3 Click **Next** from the Choose E-mail Service page, since Microsoft Exchange, POP3, IMAP or HTTP is the right option.

4 Enter your name, e-mail address and password in the Auto Account Setup window, as shown in Figure 3.2.

5 Click **Next**. Outlook searches for your server settings. It might take a few minutes to do its job. Cross your fingers that it works.

6 Click **Finish** on the Congratulations! window.

7 Click **Close**.

This should work for most POP3 and IMAP e-mail accounts. However, if it can't connect to the server, you will receive an X next to Search for [e-mail address] server settings, as shown in Figure 3.3. Your options are then to verify that you entered a valid password and to try connecting through an unencrypted connection.

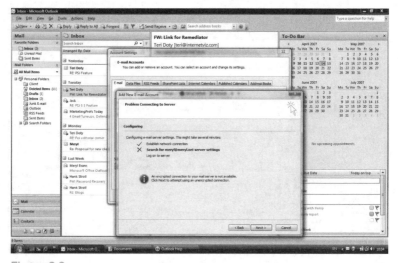

Figure 3.3
Auto Account Setup receives an error.

Creating an E-mail Account Manually

If Auto Account Setup doesn't work or you prefer to set up your e-mail account manually, do the following steps instead:

1 Select **Account Settings** from the Tools menu.

2 Click **New**.

3 Click **Next** from the Choose E-mail Service page, since Microsoft Exchange, POP3, IMAP or HTTP is the right option.

4 Check the box next to Manually configure server settings or additional server types.

5 Click **Next**.

6 Select **Internet E-mail Service**. These steps take you through setting up Internet E-mail.

Important

Microsoft Exchange option on the Choose E-mail Service page requires either checking with your IT contact person or closing Outlook, opening Control Panel and clicking the Mail icon to set up an Exchange account.

7 Fill the boxes in the Internet E-mail Settings window based on information you received from your e-mail or Internet Service Provider (ISP), as shown in Figure 3.4.

8 Click **More Settings** and select the **Outgoing Server** tab.

9 Check the box next to My outgoing server (SMTP) requires authentication. In most cases, the outgoing server requires authentication and uses the same settings as the incoming server. You may need to check with your ISP for this information.

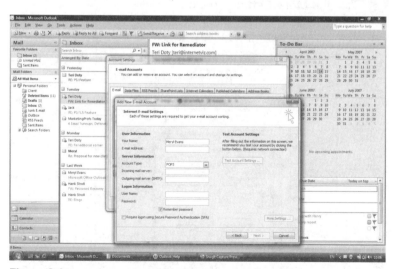

Figure 3.4

Add information regarding your e-mail account to create an Internet e-mail account.

10 Click **OK**.

11 Click **Test Account Settings** to verify the settings. If you see an **X** by any item, review the error message and check the help file or contact your ISP.

12 Click **Finish**.

> **Important**
>
> The default setting for e-mail delivery is to remove copies of messages from the server. You may be setting up an e-mail account on a laptop or other computer that isn't your primary for managing e-mails. If you download e-mail messages to the secondary computer, you won't be able to get them on the primary computer. To leave a copy of your messages on the server, do the following:

1 Select **Account Settings** from the Tools Menu.

2 Select the account and click **Change**.

3 Click the **More Settings** button.

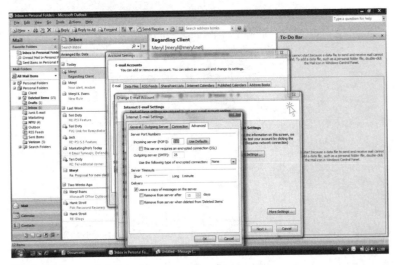

Figure 3.5
Changing e-mail settings to leave copies of messages on the server.

4 Select the **Advanced** tab.

5 Check the box next to Leave a copy of messages on the server, as shown in Figure 3.5.

You're all set. Press **F9** to send and receive e-mail messages.

3

→ Creating E-mail Messages

Chapter 2 covers the basics of creating a new e-mail message. This chapter explores more options and features. Outlook makes it possible to send and receive e-mail in one place. Many Web-based e-mail services provide information on setting up an account in an e-mail client such as Outlook. Sending a message from any account takes one click, as shown in Figure 3.6.

Formatting Text

If you're on a Microsoft Exchange server or you send e-mail messages in HTML format, you can format e-mail messages with colours, fonts, bulleted lists and other options, such as the example shown in Figure 3.7.

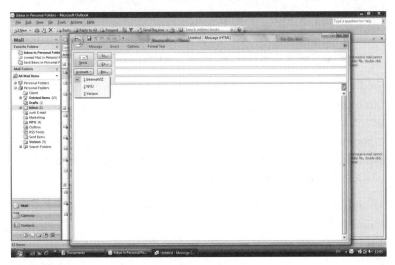

Figure 3.6
Send e-mail messages from any account in one click.

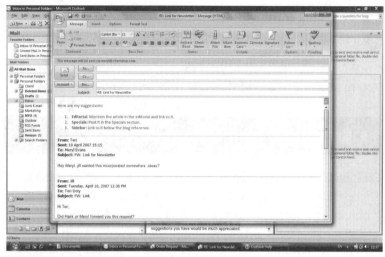

Figure 3.7
An HTML-formatted e-mail message.

Find everything you need to format a message in the Format Text tab of an e-mail message. These override the default settings, which you can set by going to the **Mail Format** tab in the Options window. Use the formatting commands as you would a Word or other electronic document. Select or highlight the text and click the command you want to apply to it.

To apply plain text formatting to every message, do the following:

1 Select **Options** from the Tools menu.

2 Select the **Mail Format** tab.

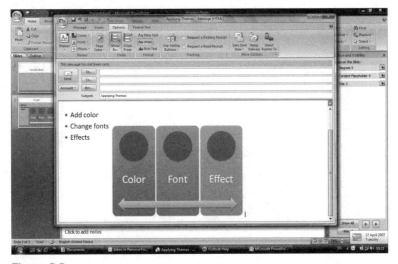

Figure 3.8
Before applying a theme to an e-mail message.

3 Select **Plain Text**.

Outlook contains a helpful formatting feature. As you move your mouse pointer over a font, colour or style, the e-mail changes to reflect the current item. The change doesn't stick unless you click the item. Move your pointer to different colours and fonts without selecting anything and see how the e-mail changes.

Microsoft Office 2007 introduces themes, which appear in all of the Office applications. You might find a theme that represents you or your organisation and wish to apply it in all documents, including e-mail.

To see Themes at work, copy and paste contents from PowerPoint, Word or another application into an e-mail message. Within the e-mail, click the **Options** tab and select a theme from **Themes**. The theme changes the look and feel of the contents in the message. Figure 3.8 shows an e-mail before applying a theme and Figure 3.9 shows the same e-mail after applying a theme.

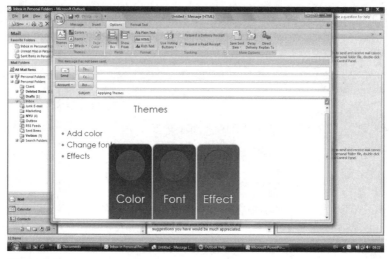

Figure 3.9
After applying a theme to an e-mail message.

Creating a Signature

You can also use the Options to create a signature to appear in every e-mail you send. You can create a signature for all new e-mail messages and another for replies and forwards. Create a new signature similar to the one shown in Figure 3.10 by doing the following:

1 Select **Options** from the Tools menu.

2 Select the **Mail Format** tab.

3 Click the **Signatures** button.

4 Click **New** and enter a name for your signature for easy recognition.

5 Enter your signature in the text box under **Edit signature**.

6 Select the name of the signature from the drop-down menu next to New messages and Replies/forwards to have the signature appear in all e-mail messages you send.

7 Click **OK**.

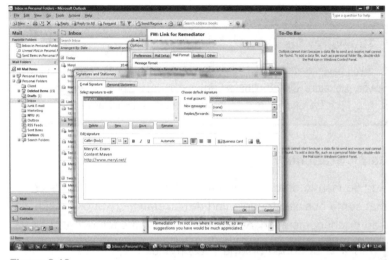

Figure 3.10

Creating and adding a new signature to appear automatically in e-mail messages.

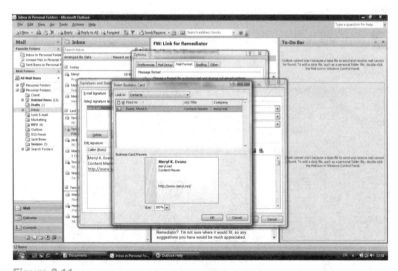

Figure 3.11

Inserting a business card into an e-mail message.

Using Stationery

Add flourish to drab e-mails with stationery. Beware, however, that some business people find e-mail stationery unprofessional. Add or change stationery themes by doing the following:

1 Select **Options** from the Tools menu.

2 Select the **Mail Format** tab.

3 Click the **Stationery and Fonts** button.

4 Click **Theme** from the Personal Stationery tab.

5 Preview and select a theme, as shown in Figure 3.12, and click **OK**.

Figure 3.12

Browse and select a theme to use in your stationery.

You can override the theme's font by clicking the arrow next to Use theme's font and selecting one of the other options that let you use your default fonts. Even if you use the theme's font, you can change it while writing the e-mail. Remember the text formatting from within the e-mail overrides the default settings.

You may have occasions when you don't want to use stationery in a message. To get rid of the stationery background, select **None** from Page Color under the Options tab in an e-mail.

Including Internet Links

Including links to websites makes it easier for the e-mail recipient to click and go to the sites. You can add a link in any of the following ways:

- Enter the link into the e-mail (e.g. *www.microsoft.com*). You don't have to use *http://* when using *www* in the link, as Figure 3.13 shows.

- Drag a link from Internet Explorer or elsewhere into the e-mail message.

Figure 3.13
Create links out of text or add as an address.

- Select the **Insert** tab from within an e-mail and click **Hyperlink** to enter a link. This displays the link.

- Select text from within the e-mail, select the **Insert** tab and click **Hyperlink** to enter a link. The selected text is clickable. This works well for long links.

Important

An Internet address that contains spaces needs its link enclosed within chevrons (<>, for example: <http://www.microsoft.com/1st Quarter Report 2007.doc> Using chevrons on all links, especially long ones, helps keep the link intact in the e-mail.

To remove a link, right-click the link and select **Remove Hyperlink**. You can also edit a link by right-clicking the link and selecting **Edit Hyperlink** as Figure 3.14 shows.

Figure 3.14
Right-click a link to edit, select, open, copy or remove the link.

Attaching Files

Thanks to viruses spreading through the Internet, users must take caution when sending and receiving attachments in e-mail messages. However, sending and receiving files through e-mail is a very useful way to share documents in their original formatting. To attach a file to an e-mail message, follow these steps:

1. Click **New** on the Standard toolbar to open a new e-mail message.

2. Click **Attach File** on the Message tab under the Include group. (Attach File also appears in the Insert tab.)

3. Locate and select your file in the Insert File window. If you have trouble finding your file in a folder, ensure that All Files appears next to the File name box.

4. Click **Insert** and the file appears in the e-mail Attached header, as shown in Figure 3.15.

5. Complete the e-mail and send it.

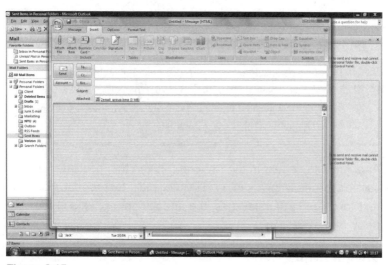

Figure 3.15
An e-mail message with a file attachment.

Timesaver tip

Attach a file or multiple files by selecting them from within a folder and dragging them into an open e-mail message in Outlook. If you can't see the e-mail message, drag the files down to the taskbar at the bottom of the screen, which opens the minimised e-mail message.

Important

Your ISP or server may have set a file size limit for files sent through e-mail. If a file is too big to send in an e-mail, try compressing the file by using a zip program, which might make it small enough, or upload the file to a free online storage service such as *www.mytempdir.com*, *www.mediamax.com* or *www.transferbigfiles.com*.

Important

Your ISP or server may prevent you from sending potentially unsafe attachments, especially those with .bat, .exe, .vbs and .js extensions. Try changing the extension to another one and inform the recipient to change it back to the original, or zip the file.

Attachments appear in the Attached box in the message headers section for messages sent in HTML or plain text format. For rich text formatted (rtf) messages, the attachment appears in the body of the message.

Saving Drafts

You may need more time to write an e-mail or have to run off for a meeting or an appointment while in the middle of writing an e-mail. Save the e-mail as a draft to ensure you don't lose it.

You can save a draft by clicking the disk icon at the top of the e-mail. If you accidentally close the e-mail, don't worry. Outlook asks whether you want to save a copy. Click **Yes** to save the e-mail to the Drafts folder. To review or open your draft message, click the **Draft** folder in the Navigation Pane to display your saved drafts.

Important

All of your sent e-mail messages appear in the Sent folder. Click the **Sent** folder in the Navigation Pane to review your messages.

→ Reading and Replying to E-mail Messages

You can control when Outlook checks for new e-mail messages, as Figure 3.16 shows. Do the following to automatically receive e-mail on a schedule:

1 Select **Options** from the Tools menu.

2 Click the **Mail Setup** tab.

3 Click **Send/Receive**.

4 Select the right Group Name.

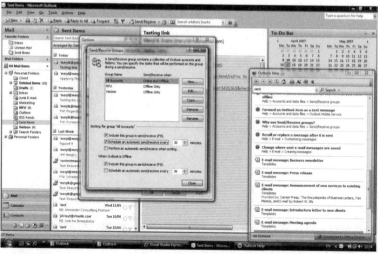

Figure 3.16

Setting Outlook to send and receive e-mail on a schedule.

5 Check the box next to **Schedule an automatic send/receive every**.

6 Enter the number of minutes (up to 1440 minutes, which is 24 hours to save you doing the maths).

7 Check the box next to **Perform an automatic send/receive when exiting**, if you want to turn on that option.

8 Click **Close**.

You can send and receive e-mail messages manually by clicking the **Send/Receive** button in the Standard toolbar or by pressing **F9**. Also, Chapter 2 covers the basics for sending, replying and forwarding e-mail messages.

Timesaver tip

If you have multiple e-mail accounts in Outlook, you can send and receive e-mail messages from a particular account. Click the arrow next to Send/Receive, select the appropriate account and click an item from its submenu (see Figure 3.17). All Accounts is fine if you have only one e-mail account in Outlook.

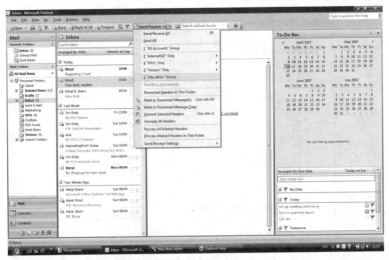

Figure 3.17
Use Send/Receive to send and receive e-mail messages for a specific account.

Organising the Inbox

Chapter 2 covers the basic views for the Reading Pane. You may prefer to sort your inbox in a different way. Outlook lets you arrange e-mail messages to appear in order by date, from, to, categories and other ways. To change the preference for sorting the inbox, do the following:

1 Select **Arrange By** from the Options menu.

2 Click your preference for sorting e-mail messages.

You can reverse the e-mail message sort order. For example, if you choose to arrange by date, you can sort e-mail messages from oldest to newest or from newest to oldest. To switch the order, click the item in the header column. For date, click **Received** once to change it. Click it again to return to the previous state.

Do you want to organise e-mail messages by groups or do you want to turn off the option? Go back to the Arrange By menu and click **Show in Groups** to organise e-mails to toggle it.

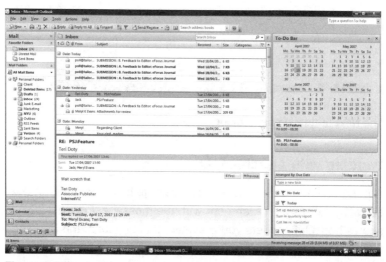

Figure 3.18
Click next to a recipient's name to see the First/Last buttons to jump to the first message in a message with many replies.

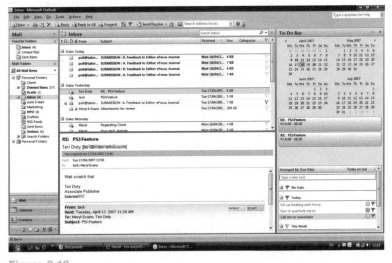

Figure 3.19

The Next button jumps to thenext reply.

Working with Attachments

A paperclip appears in the e-mail message headers in your inbox showing there's an attachment with the message. Figure 3.20 shows how Outlook lets you preview attachments in the Reading Pane. This view doesn't activate any potentially dangerous scripts. When Outlook isn't sure about an attachment, it provides a warning before letting you preview the file, as shown in Figure 3.21. Click **Preview file** to see the contents of the attachment.

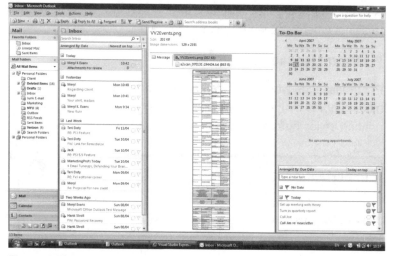

Figure 3.20

Preview attachments in the Reading Pane.

You can open an attachment by double-clicking the attachment. Once opened, you have the option of saving the file. Click **Make a Copy** from the File menu. Another way to save an attachment

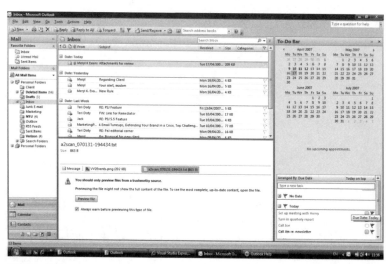

Figure 3.21

For some attachments, Outlook first displays a warning before previewing a file.

is to right-click the file name and select **Save As**. Browse Folders to select where you want to save the file and click **Save**.

Printing Messages

Print messages when you need a copy for a meeting or for making notes by hand. You can quickly print a message, change printing styles before printing and do a print preview.

> **Important**
>
> Connect your computer to a printer and ensure it's on before using printing options.

To print a copy of an e-mail message from the inbox, click the message to select it and click **Print** on the Standard toolbar. If you wish to preview the message before printing, select the message and choose **Print Preview** from the File menu.

You can change the print style while in the Print Preview window. Click **Page Setup** to change the format, paper and

Figure 3.22
Page Setup Memo Style window allows you to customise how the page appears in the printout.

header/footer, as shown in Figure 3.22. The Format tab lets you change the fonts for the title and fields, and turn shading off and on. Under the Paper tab, you can change the paper type and size, orientation and margins. Add or change the headers and footers on the print out by modifying the Header/Footer tab.

For an e-mail message that's open, click the **Office** icon in the upper-left corner and select **Print** for a list of printing options.

Forwarding Messages with Attachments

When you reply to an e-mail with an attachment, the file won't appear in the reply. However, if you forward an e-mail with an attachment, the forwarded e-mail message will contain the attachment. If you just want to forward the message and not the attachments, do the following:

1 Click **Forward** from within the e-mail or on the Standard toolbar.

2 Click the attachment to select it.

3 Click **Delete**.

Note that when you forward an e-mail, you'll need to enter a name or e-mail address into the To box. You can create a different signature to use in e-mail replies and forwards than when creating a new e-mail message.

Deleting an E-mail Message

On occasion, you may accidentally delete an e-mail you need. Thankfully, Outlook doesn't erase deleted messages for good. Instead, it moves deleted e-mail messages into the Deleted Items folder. Outlook doesn't permanently delete e-mails unless you empty the Deleted Items folder or delete the item from the folder. Restore a deleted item by opening the Deleted Items folder and moving the message into another folder.

You can delete a selected e-mail by clicking the **X** from the Standard toolbar or press the **Delete** key. For currently open e-mails, delete the message by clicking the **Delete** icon from the Actions group in the e-mail Ribbon as shown in Figure 3.23.

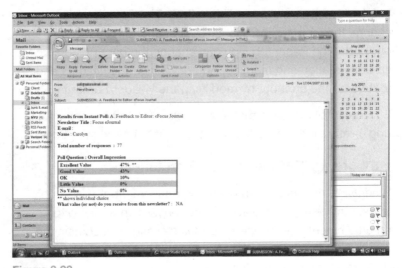

Figure 3.23
Delete an open e-mail message by clicking the big X.

To permanently delete an e-mail, do the following:

1 Open the Deleted Items folder.

2 Select the message or hold down the **Ctrl** key to select multiple messages.

3 Press **Delete**.

4 Click **Yes** when Outlook asks whether you really want to delete the item.

Go into the Navigation Pane, right-click **Deleted Items** folder and select **Empty Deleted Items** Folder to delete everything manually. If you prefer to automatically empty the Deleted Items folder every time you close Outlook, do the following:

1 Select **Options** from the Tools menu.

2 Select the **Other** tab.

3 Check the box under General next to Empty the Deleted Items folder upon exiting.

4 Click **OK**.

Next time you exit Outlook, you'll receive a message asking whether you want to delete all the items from the Deleted Items folder. This way you have some control on occasions when you may not want to empty the folder.

Saving an E-mail Message as a File

You might want to save an e-mail message as a file to edit or as a file in your document folders. You can save e-mails as HTML, text, Outlook template and Outlook Message files. Save an e-mail as a file with the following steps:

1 Select the message you wish to save and select **Save As** from the File menu.

2 Browse around the folders to where you want to save the file.

3 Change the name of the file in File Name, if needed.

4 Change the Save as Type, if needed.

Creating a Task or Appointment from a Message

One of Outlook 2007's newest features is the ability to quickly create To-Do items and appointments. Flagging is one way to turn an e-mail message into a follow-up or a reminder. From an open message, click the **Follow Up** flag icon and select the follow-up due time or click **Reminder** for setting a reminder. The new To-Do item appears in the To-Do Bar, Calendar and the Task list. Note that setting a Flag doesn't create a reminder.

Create an appointment from an e-mail message by dragging and dropping the e-mail into the correct date in the To-Do Bar's calendar. This opens a new Appointment with the e-mail message in the body. Add or change any information and save the new appointment (see Figure 3.24).

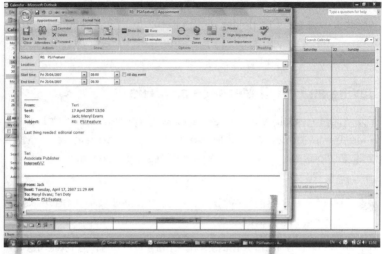

Figure 3.24

A calendar item from an e-mail message.

→ Setting E-mail Options

You can send a plain e-mail or you can add options to better manage and create effective e-mail messages. Most of the options and settings appear in the e-mail message tabs. You can also set preferred settings in Options, as shown in Figure 3.25. Access Options from the Tools menu. You can find and change the following features and options:

- **Preferences tab**: Click **E-mail Options** to change message handling and reply/forward handling options.

- **Mail Format tab**: Change the message format and HTML formatting options. Set up stationery, fonts, signatures and editor options.

- **Spelling tab**: Set spelling and autocorrection options.

- **Other tab**: Modify the settings for General, AutoArchive and Outlook Panes.

If you're not sure what settings and preferences to select, experiment with the options. You can always change them back.

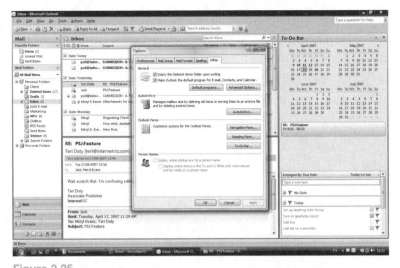

Figure 3.25

Modify e-mail preferences using the Options window.

4

Organising Your Inbox

In this lesson you'll learn how to organise your inbox using rules, folders, alerts and filters.

→ Using Rules

Do you regularly receive updates and notices? Do you want
Outlook to identify e-mails from certain people as urgent? Maybe

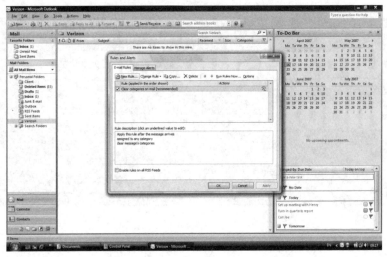

Figure 4.1
Create and edit rules from the Rules and Alerts window.

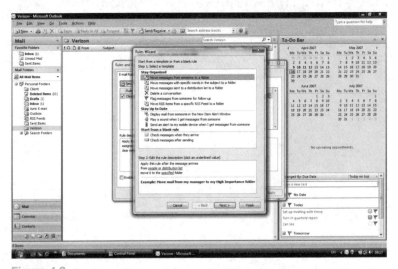

Figure 4.2
Select a template to proceed with the Rules Wizard.

you'd like to be notified when you receive an e-mail message from your manager or a family member. Rules help you keep your inbox organised and alert you to important items. There are endless combinations of rules you can create. Figures 4.1 and 4.2 show examples of creating rules.

Moving an E-mail to a Specific Folder

The following steps show you how to move an e-mail with a specific address into a specific folder. Once you do these steps, you will be able to modify this rule to do many things.

1. Select **Rules and Alerts** from the Tools menu.

2. Click **New Rule**.

3. Select **Move messages from someone to a folder** and click **Next**.

4. Leave **from people or distribution list** checked, as shown in Figure 4.3.

5. Click **people or distribution list** in the Step 2 window.

6. Search for the name if it's in your Address Book. If

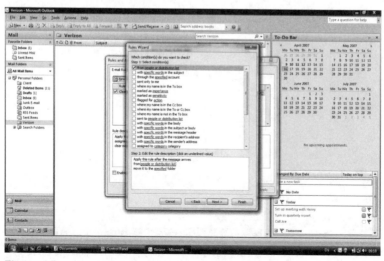

Figure 4.3

Select the conditions on which the rule should act.

not, enter the e-mail address into the **From** box and click
OK.

7 Leave **move it to the specified folder** checked.

8 Click **specified** in the Step 2 window.

9 Select the folder or click **New** to create a new folder, as
Figure 4.4 shows. Enter a name into the **Name** box for the
new folder, click **OK** to exit the Create New Folder window,
and click **Next** to go to the Exceptions window.

10 Click **Next** on the Exceptions window.

11 Enter a name for the rule that helps you identify the rule and
its purpose.

12 Check or uncheck the box in Step 2, depending on whether
you want to run the rule now for messages already in your
inbox.

13 Leave **Turn on this rule** checked and click **Finish**.

14 Click **OK**.

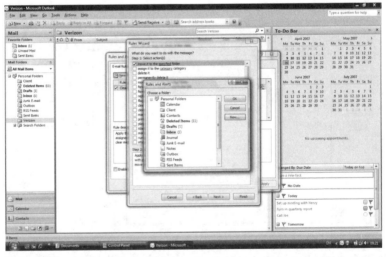

Figure 4.4
Select the folder where Outlook should move items meeting the rule's
conditions.

Use the same steps to move e-mail from e-mail newsletters into a folder. If you have multiple e-mail accounts in Outlook, you could use this rule to file e-mails to folders for each e-mail address. For example, you may have personal and business e-mail accounts set up in Outlook. Change Steps 4, 5 and 6 to the following:

1 Uncheck fr**om people or distribution list** and check **with specific words in the recipient's address**.

2 Click **people or distribution** list in the Step 2 window.

3 Enter your e-mail address in the **From** box and click **OK**.

4 Follow Steps 7–14 to finish setting the rule.

Changing an Existing Rule

You may need to change or add information to an existing rule. The following steps add another specific word to a rule that moves arriving e-mail into a specific folder:

1 Select **Rules and Alerts** from the Tools menu.

2 Click **Change Rules** and select **Edit Rule Settings** from the dropdown list.

3 Click the underlined keyword.

4 Enter another keyword, click **Add** and click **OK**, as shown in Figure 4.5.

5 Click **Finish**.

6 Click **Run Rules Now**.

7 Check the box of the rule to run.

8 Click **Run Now**.

9 Click **Close** and **OK** to close the Rules and Alerts window.

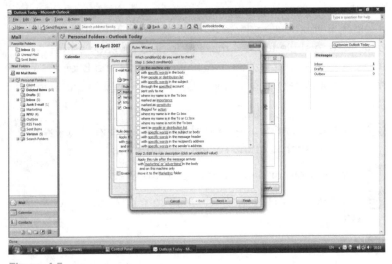

Figure 4.5
Adding another keyword to an existing rule.

Creating an Alert

Alert rules known as Stay Up to Date operate in the same way as the Stay Organized rules. Alerts can do the following:

■ Pop up in a New Item Alerts window.

■ Play a sound when an e-mail arrives.

■ Send an alert to a mobile device.

Figure 4.6 shows an example of a New Item alert. The steps for creating the rule are the same, except you select one of the three items from the Stay Up to Date list on the Rules Wizard.

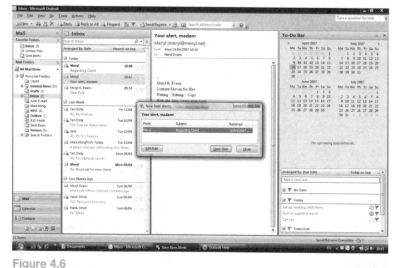

Figure 4.6

A New Item alert.

→ Using Filters

It doesn't take much time before Outlook folders contain hundreds of messages, making searching for a specific message rather challenging. Filtering items and files makes your search easier as it displays only items that contain what you need.

Sorting, on the other hand, doesn't cut down the clutter. Instead, it changes the order in which the messages appear. If you have 100 messages in a folder, sorting rearranges the 100 messages. Filtering lowers the number of messages you see based on your filter settings. Instead of looking through 100 messages, it cuts down the number of messages to scan, helping you find what you need. To use filtering, do the following (see Figure 4.7):

1 Select **Current View** from the View menu.

2 Select **Customize Current View**.

3 Click **Filter**.

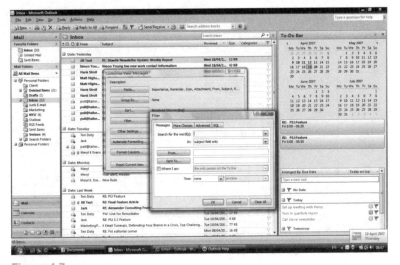

Figure 4.7

Use Filter to find messages.

The Messages tab of the Filter window offers options for searching by keywords in the subject field, message body and frequently used text fields. Click **From** to see the Contacts list and select a name from the list or enter an e-mail address into the box. Sent To works in the same way as From. You can also narrow down your results by whether you're the only person addressed in the e-mail, or one of several people, and by time. You can use one, some or all of the options.

The More Choices tab can search for messages from a specific category as well as the following (see Figure 4.8):

■ Unread or read items.

■ Items with or without attachments.

■ Importance: normal, high or low.

■ Marked as completed, flagged by someone else, with no flag or flagged by you.

■ Match case: using a common word such as "you" turns up many results. Matching the case for "You" or "you" can cut the number of results.

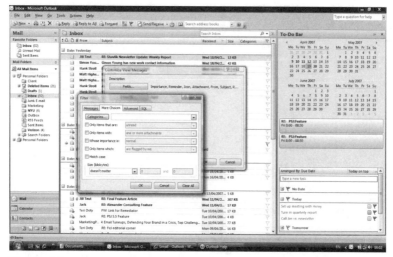

Figure 4.8

Add more filtering conditions with the More Choices tab.

■ Size: you may remember whether the message was short or long, which can help narrow your results.

The Advanced tab lets you customise your filter criteria. To customise a filter, take the following steps:

1 Click the **Advanced** tab in the Filter window, as shown in Figure 4.9.

2 Select **Field**.

3 Select an item from the Field list and click the submenu item you want, as Figure 4.9 shows.

4 Select an item from the **Value** drop-down list.

5 Click **Add to List**.

6 Repeat Steps 4 and 5 until you select all the criteria (see Figure 4.10).

7 Click **OK** twice.

To remove a filter, select **Current View** from the Customize Current View menu, and click Filter and **Clear All**.

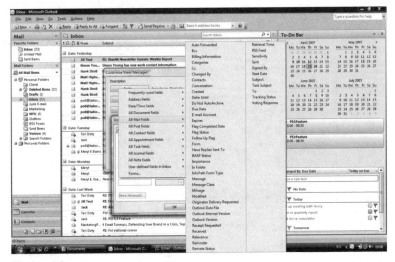

Figure 4.9

Select from a list of fields to create an advanced filter.

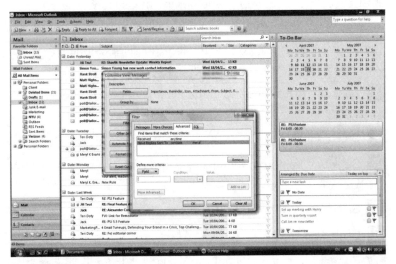

Figure 4.10

Add additional criteria using the items in Filter's Advanced tab.

→ Managing Folders

E-mail organisation experts recommend keeping the number of messages in your inbox low. This doesn't mean deleting them. Instead, move them into folders with a structure that works for you. You can find the folders in the Navigation Pane under either Personal Folders or Mailbox. You can also access the Folder List by clicking the Folder icon at the bottom of the Navigation Pane. Click the plus sign to expand the list and the minus sign to collapse the list.

Creating Folders

If you work with multiple clients and need to organise information by client, creating a folder for each client might work well. Another way is to create a folder called Clients and create subfolders under Client for each client. The following shows how to create a new folder (see Figure 4.11):

1 Select **New** and **Folder** from the File menu, or use the **Ctrl+Shift+E** shortcut.

Figure 4.11
Create a new folder.

2 Enter a name for the folder in the Name box.

3 Leave Mail and Post Items as the selected item in Folder contains.

4 Select the item where you want the folder created.

5 Click **OK**.

To create a subfolder in the new folder, do the following:

1 Right-click the name of the new folder.

2 Select **New Folder** (see Figure 4.12).

3 Enter a name for the folder in the Name box.

4 Leave Mail and Post Items as the selected item in Folder contains.

5 Confirm the new folder appears highlighted.

6 Click **OK**.

Figure 4.12
Select the folder where the subfolder should go.

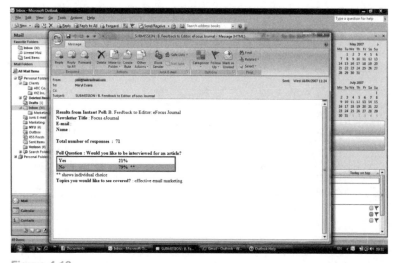

Figure 4.13
Move an e-mail message to a folder.

Moving Messages into Folders

A folder doesn't have to exist when you want to move a message into a new folder. You can create the folder with the message open. Do the following to move the message into a new folder:

1 Click **Move to Folder** from the Actions group, as shown in Figure 4.13.

2 Click **Other Folder**.

3 Click **New** in the Move Item to window, as Figure 4.14 shows.

4 Enter a name for the folder in the Name box.

5 Leave Mail and Post Items as the selected item in Folder contains.

6 Select the item where you want the folder created.

7 Click **OK**.

To move a message into an existing folder, click **Move to Folder** from the message's Ribbon and select the folder name. You can

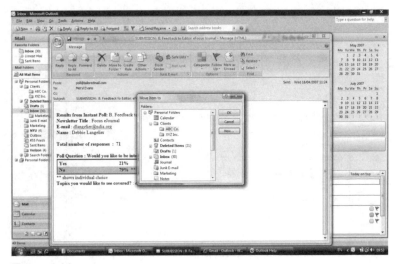

Figure 4.14
Create a new folder.

also drag the message from the inbox or folder and drop it into the desired folder.

Categorising Messages by Colour

Colour categories provide a visual tool to aid in quickly finding relevant messages. Create and name categories to identify messages related to meetings and contacts. Assign a colour to messages of business or personal nature. Give major projects their own colours to better manage and organise the project information throughout Outlook, since colour categories work with Calendar, Contacts and Tasks. For more on colour categories, see Chapter 11. You can assign as many categories to an item as you need.

Right-click any message, select Categorize and pick the category to instantly apply the new category to the selected message, or click **All Categories** to assign more than one category or to modify, add, delete or rename the categories. Figure 4.15 shows a list of categories.

Figure 4.15

Select All Categories to modify or select multiple categories.

Click the category icon 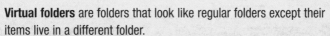 in the Standard toolbar to access the categories list.

→ Using Search Folders

Search folders create virtual folders with items matching the search criteria. You can search folders e-mails from a specific individual. The results from this search appear in a single folder, even though the actual messages live in other folders.

Jargon buster

Virtual folders are folders that look like regular folders except their items live in a different folder.

Outlook comes with three default search folders: Categorized Mail, Large Mail (messages over 100 kB in size) and Unread Mail.

Click these at any time in the Navigation Pane for a list of messages. Note the Unread Mail folder lists all unread messages not just those in the inbox.

Timesaver tip

To customise an existing search folder, right-click the folder, select **Customize this Search Folder** and click **Criteria**.

Take the following steps to create a new search folder:

1 Click the arrow next to New in the Standard tool bar and select **Search Folder**, or use the **Ctrl+Shift+P** shortcut.

2 Select a Search Folder from the list, as shown in Figure 4.16.

3 Select the folders to search mail (if you have multiple personal folders).

4 Click **OK**, and the results should appear as in Figure 4.17.

Figure 4.16

Create a New Search Folder.

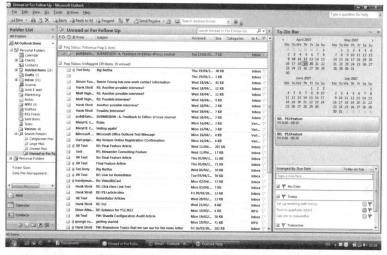

Figure 4.17
Outlook displays the Search Folder results.

Important

Deleting the Search Folder doesn't delete the messages contained in that folder from their original locations. However, if you delete more than one open or selected messages appearing in a Search Folder, then Outlook deletes them from their original folders.

→ Archiving E-mail Messages

No matter how well you organise a mailbox, you will likely need to store older messages in order to conserve storage space. Archiving messages sent and received before a specific date works for messages that you need to keep but use rarely. Outlook archives old items to an archive file and deletes expired items, or both.

Outlook turns on AutoArchive by default to automatically archive old items on a set schedule. Outlook archives the following items:

- Outbox items older than three months.

- Sent and deleted items older than two months.

- All other items, including the Inbox, Calendar, Tasks, Notes, Journals and Drafts older than six months.

To modify AutoArchive settings, do the following:

1 Click **Options** from the Tools menu.

2 Select the **Other** tab.

3 Click **AutoArchive**.

4 Select and change the options you want for AutoArchive, as Figure 4.18 shows.

5 Click **Apply these settings to all folders now** to apply the new options to all folders. This overrides any custom archive settings applied to individual folders.

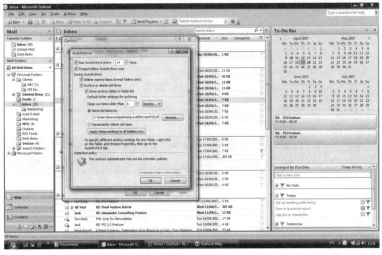

Figure 4.18
Changing AutoArchive options.

Set AutoArchives for individual folders by doing the following steps:

1 Right-click the folder to change its settings, and click **Properties**.

2 Select the **AutoArchive** tab.

3 Decide whether to archive the folder. If not, select **Do not archive items in this folder** and click **Apply**. If you want to archive this folder, go to Step 4.

4 Decide whether to apply the default AutoArchive settings or to archive the folder using the settings you set.

5 Click **Apply**.

6 Click **OK**.

Manually run AutoArchive using the following steps:

1 Click **Archive** from the File menu.

2 Select to archive all folders based on AutoArchive settings or Archive a specific folder, as shown in Figure 4.19.

3 Enter the date to archive items sent and received before the selected date.

4 Complete the remaining settings based on your preferences.

5 Click **OK**.

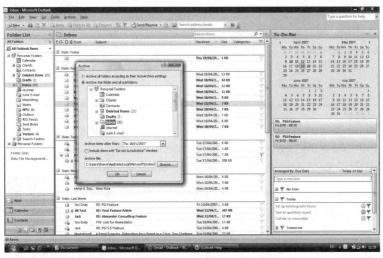

Figure 4.19
Setting up manual archiving.

Restore archived items back to their original folders by following these steps:

1 Select **Import and Export** from the File menu.

2 Click **Import from another program or file**.

3 Click **Next**.

4 Select **Personal Folder File (.pst)** and click **Next**.

5 Change the file name from backup.pst to the name of the archive file to import.

6 Select the folder to import from and click **Include subfolders**, if preferred.

7 Select how you want Outlook to handle duplicates.

8 Click **Import items into the same folder in**, and click the folders with the same name as the folders from which you import.

9 Click **Finish**.

Jargon buster

Personal Folders File (.pst) is a file on your hard disk with a .pst extension that contains your Outlook data, including messages, files, forms, contacts and appointments. The default location for the .pst file lives here:
drive:\Documents and Settings*user*\Local Settings\Application Data\Microsoft\Outlook.

To restore archived items to a new folder, create the new folder and follow the previously outlined steps, except for Step 8. Instead, click **Import items into the current folder**.

Important

Back up your .pst file regularly because you can't recover the file if it becomes corrupt. Better still, save it to a backup drive or use an online storage service.

As you delete items from your Deleted Items folder, the size of the Personal Folders file (.pst) won't change unless you compact the file. Compacting the file restores hard disk space and improves Outlook's performance.

4

Important

Outlook won't compact items deleted from a folder. It compacts items only from the Deleted Items folder. Outlook also requires the personal folders file to be 16 kB or larger and to have at least 16 kB of space in order to do a compact.

To compact the Personal Folders file, do the following:

1 Select **Data File Management** from the File menu.

2 Select the data file you want to compact.

3 Click **Settings**.

4 Click **Compact Now**, as shown in Figure 4.20.

Figure 4.20

Compact folders to conserve disk space.

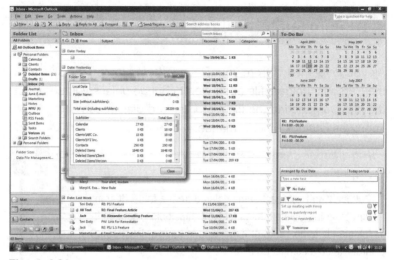

Figure 4.21

Viewing folder sizes.

5 Click **OK** and **Close** to return to Mail.

It may take Outlook a few minutes to do the compacting.

Timesaver tip

To view folder sizes quickly, click the **Folders** icon at the bottom of your Navigation Pane, as shown in Figure 4.21, and click **Folder Sizes**.

→ Cleaning Up with Mailbox Cleanup Tool

The Mailbox Cleanup tool shows the size of your folders, archives older items and empties the Deleted Items folder. It doesn't compact the folder. View Mailbox Cleanup by selecting **Mailbox Cleanup** from the Tools menu. The tool can do the following:

▓ Display the size of your mailbox and folders shown in Figure 4.22.

- Find items by age or size.

- Run AutoArchive to move old items to the archive file on the computer.

- View the size of and empty the Deleted Items folder.

- Delete alternative versions of items in your mailbox and View Conflicts Size. This applies only when items conflict on an Exchange Server account with synchronisation issues. Outlook creates a folder called Conflicts when this occurs.

Running this tool occasionally optimises Outlook's performance.

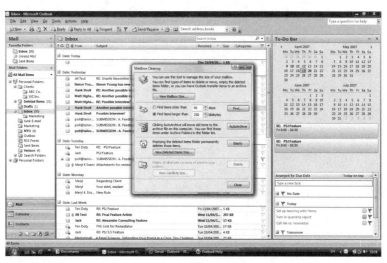

Figure 4.22
Manage the size of the mailbox with the Mailbox Cleanup tool.

5

Using the To-Do Bar

In this lesson you'll be introduced to the To-Do Bar and learn how to work with Tasks.

→ Introducing the To-Do Bar

The biggest to-do in Outlook 2007 is the addition of the To-Do Bar. Although Outlook Today provides an overview of your day, the To-Do Bar integrates all of Outlook's features and takes up less space, as shown in Figure 5.1. With the To-Do Bar, you can get right to work on almost anything without changing the view. The To-Do Bar contains the current month's calendar, your next three appointments and a list of your current tasks.

About the only thing you could do in Outlook Today is check off a completed task. The rest required clicking an item to change or delete it as shown in Figure 5.2. Furthermore, Outlook Today took up the whole window. The To-Do Bar takes up little space on the right-hand side and you can minimise it with one click on the >> at the top of the To-Do Bar. Figure 5.3 shows how the To-Do Bar appears when minimised: it then displays your next appointment and the number of tasks due for the day.

Figure 5.1

To-Do Bar occupies less than 25 per cent of Outlook's window.

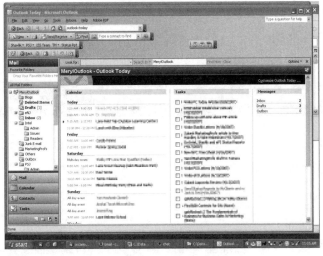

Figure 5.2

Outlook Today's screen in Windows XP.

The To-Do Bar appears in Mail, Task, Contact and Notes views.
You can minimise and maximise with a click, or you can turn it
off by doing the following:

1 Click **View**.

Figure 5.3

To-Do Bar minimised.

2 Select **To-Do Bar**.

3 Select **Off**.

→ Customising the To-Do Bar

The To-Do Bar contains three parts that you can turn off and on:

- Date Navigator.
- Appointments.
- Task List.

The Task List isn't limited to the items you enter in Tasks. It also contains flagged e-mails and notes. You can drag these items into the To-Do Bar to turn them into To-Do items.

Jargon buster

To-do items are anything flagged for follow-up, including e-mail messages, tasks and contacts. **Tasks** are items created in Outlook to track from start to finish. To-do items are not always tasks, but tasks are always to-do items.

Turning off Date Navigator, Appointments or To-Do moves up the other content in the bar and creates more white space. You can fill the white space by increasing the number of to-do items and rows of months. Access Options to change the view by doing the following:

1 Click **View**.

2 Select **To-Do Bar**.

3 Select **Options**.

To-Do Bar Options lets you select which items to display in the bar (see Figure 5.4). Date Navigator's Number of Month Rows

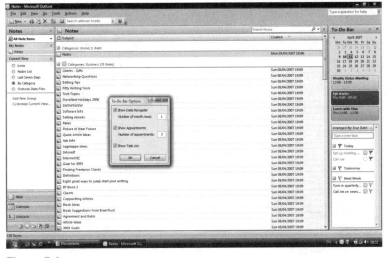

Figure 5.4

The To-Do Bar Options box.

represents one month when the To-Do Bar appears in its default
size. Enter **2** to view the current and next months in the To-Do
Bar. You can display up to nine rows' worth of months.

Widen the To-Do Bar to view more months per row, as Figure 5.5
shows. Move the cursor to the left edge of the To-Do Bar until
the cursor changes and drag the cursor to change the size. The
To-Do Bar can go as far as half of the screen. Scroll through past
and future months by clicking on the blue arrows next to the
month in the first row.

Timesaver tip

Right-click the To-Do Bar title bar to access its options.

For Show Appointments, enter the number of appointments you
wish to view in the To-Do Bar. The default is 3, and the
maximum is 25 appointments.

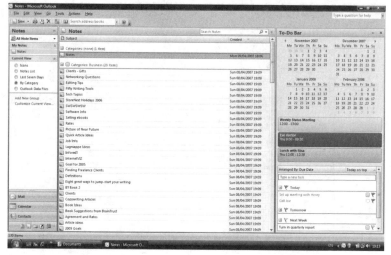

Figure 5.5

The wider the To-Do Bar, the more months it displays in the selected number of rows.

→ Working with To-Do Items

Most people assume a checkbox next to a task is for ticking off a completed task. This isn't the case in the To-Do Bar's Task List, unless you Set Quick Click. The box next to the task identifies its category. When clicked, the box changes colours, depending on the Set Quick Click settings. No category is the default, and clicking on it changes a coloured box to white to indicate that the task doesn't have a category.

Jargon buster

Set Quick Click lets you change the setting of an item to take action when single clicking the item. For example, using Set Quick Click for the Flags column in the Task List lets you change the option to click once on a Flag to modify its due date or delete it, depending on its status.

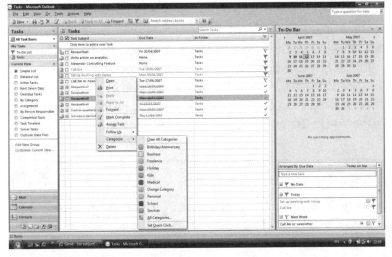

Figure 5.6
Change options with Set Quick Click.

Assigning Categories to To-Do Items

If you frequently use one category, change the category Quick Click setting to that category. Take the following steps to change the category (see Figure 5.6):

1 Right-click category box.

2 Select **Set Quick Click**.

3 Select your most frequently used category.

4 Click **OK**.

After changing the Quick Click, the category will change between no category and your selected category each time you click the box.

Deleting To-Do Bar Items

Outlook removes an item from the To-Do Bar in one of the following two ways:

■ **Marked complete**: Upon checking a task as complete,

Outlook removes the item from the To-Do Bar. The item remains in the To-Do List and Tasks list as a completed item.

■ **Cleared flag:** Clearing a flag on an item means the task no longer has time constraints. Outlook removes it from the To-Do Bar and the To-Do List. The item remains in its original location. For example, an e-mail with a cleared flag no longer appears in the To-Do Bar or To-Do List, but it still shows up in Mail.

Important

The To-Do Bar Task List has a quirk: you cannot clear flags from To-Do items entered in Tasks, but you can clear flags for tasks from e-mails, contacts and notes. Right-click the flag next to a task to access its options.

To remove an item from the To-Do Bar, right-click it to open the menu, and then do one of the following (see Figure 5.7):

■ Select **Follow Up** and then click **Mark Complete**. This identifies an item as complete.

Figure 5.7

Right-click a task to delete it, mark as complete or change the follow-up option.

- Select **Follow Up** and click **Clear Flag** to clear a flag. See the Important box opposite regarding clearing flags.

- Click **Delete** from the shortcut menu to delete the item.

Take care when deleting an item, as Outlook may delete it from elsewhere, as explained in the following Important box.

Important

When you use Clear Flag or Delete Task, or you check a task as complete, Outlook retains a record of the item. However, if you choose Delete Item, the item disappears from Outlook for good. Using Delete Item on a flagged e-mail deletes the e-mail not only from the task list but also from the inbox.

→ Viewing Tasks

Since Outlook 2007 integrates Tasks, Mail, Calendar and Contacts better, it provides more ways to view tasks and to-do items. Tasks appear in three main locations: To-Do Bar, Tasks and Calendar.

To-Do Bar

By default, the To-Do Bar appears in most Outlook views, providing an easy way to view the most current Tasks. Refer to the To-Do Bar introduction at the start of this chapter to learn about customising its views.

Tasks

Open Tasks by clicking the clipboard icon at the bottom of the Navigation Pane to view the tasks (see Figure 5.8). With Tasks open, you can quickly change the Tasks settings by selecting a different option from the Current View in the Navigation Pane. Click **Customize Current View** to customise the currently selected view.

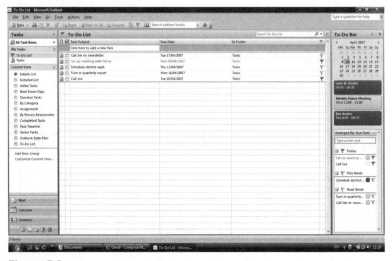

Figure 5.8

The Task List view.

Calendar

The Daily Task List shows only in the Day and Week views of Calendar (see Figure 5.9). Tasks appear at the bottom of Calendar. Tasks can appear on their start dates or due dates. To

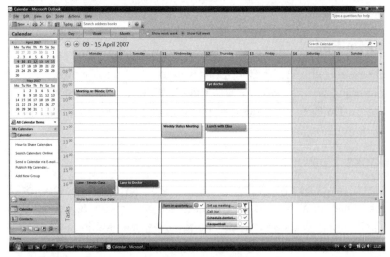

Figure 5.9

The Daily Task List appears below the Calendar.

change this option, right-click **Show tasks on**: and select your preference.

The Day view lists the task, start and due dates, reminder time and folder location. The Week view shows only the Task name. Modify the Daily Task List view by doing these steps:

1 Click **Daily Task List** on the View menu.

2 Select **Normal**, **Minimized**, **Off** or **Arrange By**.

If you select Arrange By, your choices are By Start Date and By Due Date. This menu also lets you turn on and off the showing of completed tasks.

Jargon buster

Daily Task List is the name of the Tasks appearing in Calendar. It doesn't say Daily Task List anywhere in Calendar, but Outlook's menus and Help file use the term.

→ Creating a New Task

Any time you create a new task, Outlook flags it for follow-up, even when a task has no start and finish dates. Like any other feature in Outlook, you can create a new task in various ways. The fastest way to enter a new task is to type the task into the To-Do Bar where it says **Type a new task**. The following are other ways to create a new task:

■ Click **New** from the File menu, and select **Task**.

■ Use the shortcut **Ctrl+Shift+K**.

■ Enter the task into the text box at the top of the Task window that says **Click here to add a new Task**.

■ On the bottom of Calendar view in the Tasks, click a blank space and type in a new task.

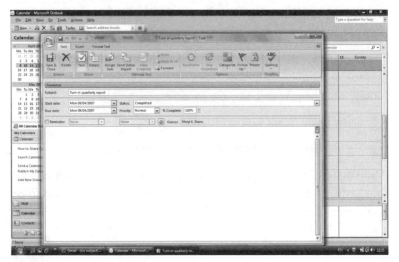

Figure 5.10

The Task window contains options for managing the task.

■ Drag an item, such as an e-mail message or contact, to the Tasks icon at the bottom of the Navigation Pane. This immediately opens a new task window, where you can fill in the rest of the details.

Timesaver tip

Move a task to another day in the Calendar by dragging and dropping the task to the new date.

Right-click a task and select **Open** to add more details, including the start and due dates, status, percentage complete, priority, notes, categories, follow-up and reminders (see Figure 5.10). You can also set the task's recurrence and assign it to others from this window.

→ Creating a Recurring Task

Recurring tasks can happen daily, twice-weekly, weekly, monthly, on the third Monday of each month, yearly, every four years (the World Cup and the Olympics) ... To make a task recur, do the following steps from the open Task window:

1 Click **Recurrence**.

2 Select the frequency of the recurrence pattern: **Daily**, **Weekly**, **Monthly** or **Yearly** (see Figure 5.11).

3 Complete the Recurrence pattern based on the task recurrence preferences.

4 Select **Regenerate new task** if you want a new task to appear as soon as you mark the task complete.

5 Click **OK** to close the Task Recurrence window.

Regenerate new task means that the next task won't appear until you've marked the previous task as complete. For example,

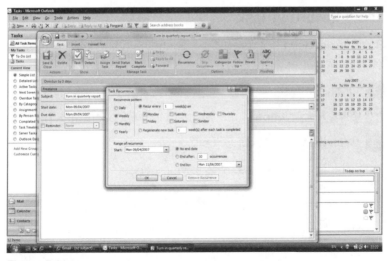

Figure 5.11
Options for a recurring task.

you create a new task to remind you to send a status report to your boss every Friday. If you complete the task on Thursday and mark it as complete, the next one appears even though you have finished the report one day early.

On the other hand, if you want to create a task to remind you to exercise on Monday, Wednesday and Friday, and you want a reminder on Wednesday even though you didn't exercise on Monday, do not select **Regenerate new task**.

Skip a Recurring Task Occurrence

Occasionally, you may want to skip an occurrence of a recurring task. For example, you might need to cancel an occurrence because of a holiday; in this case, you don't want to delete all of the occurrences, just one. To delete a recurring task occurrence, take the following steps:

1 Open the recurrence you want to skip.

2 Click **Skip Recurrence** on the Task tab in the Options group.

3 Click **Remove Recurrence**.

End a Recurring Task

Some tasks don't last forever, so delete them and keep your task list free of clutter. Here are the steps to end a recurring task:

1 Open the recurring task.

2 Click **Recurrence** in the Task tab in the Options group.

3 Click **Remove Recurrence**.

That task is now one less thing to worry about.

→ Assigning Tasks to Others

Although you may assign a task to someone else, you may wish to stay updated on its progress. Or perhaps the person who originally received a task delegates it to someone else. You can remain in the loop on the task's progress and receive a notification when it's completed. Task assignments also help when you may need to reassign a task because the recipient declined or can't complete it for other reasons. To assign a task, do the following (see Figure 5.12 on next page):

1. From the File menu, select **New** and **Task Request**, or use the shortcut **Ctrl+Shift+U**.

2. Enter the recipient's e-mail address or name in the To box.

3. Enter the name for the task in the Subject box.

4. Set the dates, status and priority options.

5. Check or uncheck the boxes for Keep an updated copy of this task on my task list and Send me a status report when this task is complete, based on your preferences.

Important

For recurring tasks, the task remains in your task list without you receiving updates. If you choose to receive a status report, you receive a status report each time the recurring task is complete.

6. Enter additional information into the body of the Task, if needed.

7. Click **Send**.

Important

A person who declines an assigned task still owns the task until you return the task to your task list.

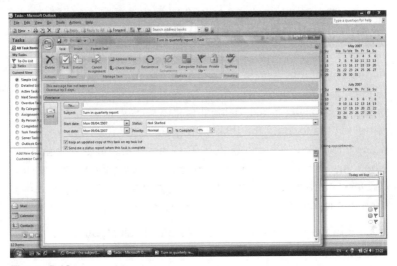

Figure 5.12

Assigning a task resembles creating an e-mail message.

Assigning an Existing Task

Assigning and forwarding tasks work well if you're on an Exchange server. Someone who isn't on Exchange will receive the task request by e-mail. However, the only way to get an update on the status is for the recipient to send you an e-mail message regarding the progres of the task; updates aren't automatic.

To assign an existing task, do the following:

1. From the Task list, open the task you want to assign by clicking it twice.

2. Click **Assign Task**.

3. Enter the recipient's e-mail address or name in the To box.

4. Modify the name of the task in the Subject box, if needed.

5. Set the dates, status and priority options.

6. Check or uncheck the boxes for Keep an updated copy of this task on my task list and Send me a status report when this task is complete, based on your preferences.

7 Enter additional information into the body of the Task, if needed.

8 Click **Send**.

Forwarding a Task

Forwarding a task works similarly to assigning a task. Instead of clicking **Assign Task**, click **Forward**.

Reclaiming a Task

You can reclaim a sent task even if the recipient has yet to accept or decline it. The steps to reclaim a task, rejected or not, are as follows:

1 Open the Sent folder in Mail to locate the task.

2 Open the message.

3 Click **Return to Task List** in the Manage Task group.

> **Important**
>
> If you can't find Return to Task List in your e-mail message, you're most likely not on a server that can take advantage of this feature.

→ Completing a Task

Checking off a task as completed or no longer needing follow-up feels refreshing. Once marked completed, the task no longer appears as an active task in Outlook. You can mark a task as complete in any of the following ways:

- Click the flag icon next to the item in the To-Do Bar, Tasks or Daily Task List in Calendar.

- Right-click the task and select **Mark Complete** from the shortcut menu.

- Double-click the task and enter **100** in the % Complete box.

To mark as complete e-mail messages marked with the follow-up flag, you can open the e-mail and click **Mark Complete**.

Go ahead and celebrate completing the task!

Deleting a Task

In some instances, you may not need to do the task at all. Rather than making a record of completing a deleted or cancelled task by checking it off, delete it. Right-click the task and click **Delete**.

Recovering or Restoring a Task

Typically, it's not possible to restore a task unless Outlook is on Exchange or comes with Business Contact Manager. In Business Contact Manager, you can find deleted tasks in Deleted Items under Business Contact Manager in the Navigation Pane.

Jargon buster

Business Contact Manager comes as part of Microsoft Office Small Business 2007, Office Professional 2007, Office Ultimate 2007 and Office Enterprise 2007 editions. It provides small businesses with features to manage client relationships, opportunities and projects.

→ Printing Tasks

You can print a list of tasks or individual tasks. The list of tasks prints the task, due date, folder location and flag column. Printing an individual task not only includes the same information in a printed list, but also contains the status, percentage complete, total and actual work, owner and categories.

To print an individual task, right-click the task and select **Print**. To print a list of tasks, take the following steps (see Figure 5.13):

1. Open Tasks.

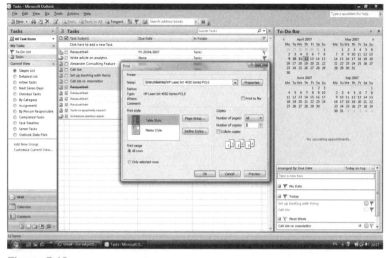

Figure 5.13
Print a task or list of tasks.

2 Select **Print** from the File menu.

3 Select **Table Style** or **Memo Style**. To see how each style looks, click **Preview** in the Print window.

You can select specific tasks to print instead of printing the whole list or a single task. Hold down the **Ctrl** key while clicking the tasks you wish to select. Then select **Print** from the File menu and select **Only selected rows** under Print Range.

Timesaver tip

To select a group of Tasks, click the first task. Hold down the **Shift** key and then click the last task. Outlook highlights all the tasks between the first and last tasks. Both this and using the **Ctrl** key to select specific items work for many lists, including contacts, appointments, e-mails and notes.

Managing Calendar

In this lesson you'll learn all about working with the calendar including how to add items, create appointments, share calendars and work with meeting requests.

→ Managing Calendar Views

To access the Calendar module, click **Calendar** in the Navigation
Pane. The Calendar module contains the Date Navigator for
switching dates quickly, options for sharing, searching and
publishing Calendars, and the To-Do Bar. At the top of the
Calendar, click **Day**, **Week** or **Month** to switch views. The Back
and Forward navigation buttons appear just below these views to
navigate to the previous and next day, week or month in the
calendar.

Jargon buster

Date Navigator is the small calendar that appears to the left of the
current Calendar view, as shown in Figure 6.1. Click any date in the
Date Navigator to switch to the selected date.

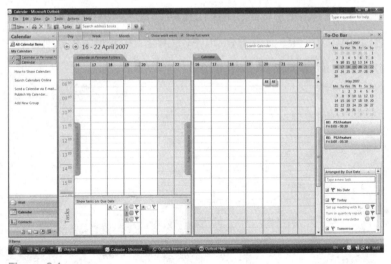

Figure 6.1
The new Calendar interface makes it easy to jump to another date and
find items.

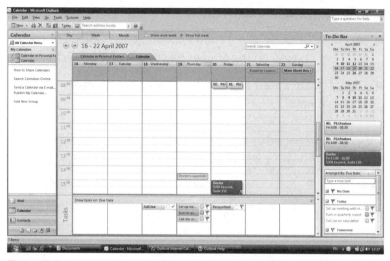

Figure 6.2
Click the tab to view two calendars in overlay mode.

Outlook 2007 introduces the ability to view two or more calendars side by side in Calendar. You can view multiple calendars by day, week or month. In the Navigation Pane, click the checkbox of each calendar you want to view to see them side by side.

You can also view calendars in overlay mode. Again, go into Navigation Pane and check the calendars you want to view. Click the arrow in the calendar's tab, and the calendars overlap, as shown in Figure 6.2. Overlay another calendar by clicking its arrow on the tab. The items in the Calendar on the back tab appear lighter, while the ones in the front tab appear darker. Remove a Calendar from Overlay by clicking its tab.

For the Week view, you can view only Monday to Friday for the week by clicking **Show work week** or you can display all seven days by clicking **Show full week**. These tabs appear next to the Day, Week and Month tabs. Click the **Month** tab to switch to Month view. You can indicate whether you want to view details on the calendar, as Figure 6.3 shows. The three detail choices are as follows:

- **Low**: Displays only events.

- **Medium**: Displays events and appointments, which appear as solid bars based on the time of day they're scheduled.

- **High**: Displays start and end time for all events and appointments.

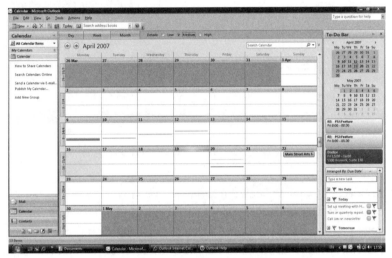

Figure 6.3

In the Month view, the Medium detail shows bars for scheduled Appointments and the names of the Events.

→ Adding Items in Calendar

Calendar contains four different types of item. Each item appears in a different place on Calendar and contains information specific to its type. The four items are:

- Appointment.

- Event.

- Meeting.

- Task.

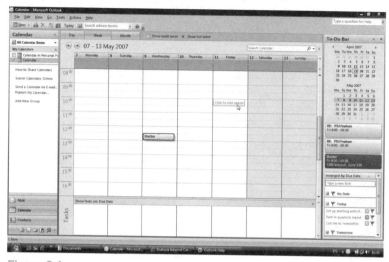

Figure 6.4

Select the time to enter a new appointment.

Creating an Appointment

An appointment is an activity you do alone at a scheduled time without creating a meeting request, as shown in Figure 6.4. To enter an appointment, jump to the date of the appointment. Move the pointer to the start time and double-click to enter the details of the appointment, including the Subject, Location, Start and End dates and times. Click **Save & Close**.

Timesaver tip

You can quickly create a new appointment without opening the appointment window. Move the pointer to the appointment start time on the calendar and enter the relevant details.

Do you need to reschedule the appointment? Simply drag and drop the appointment to the new time, as shown in Figure 6.5.

Make an appointment longer or shorter by moving the pointer over the bottom of the appointment until you see the two-sided

Figure 6.5

Move the appointment to a new time.

arrow cursor, as shown in Figure 6.6. Click and stretch or shrink the appointment time.

Colleagues can review the availability of meeting attendees by checking the status on the shared calendar to see whether

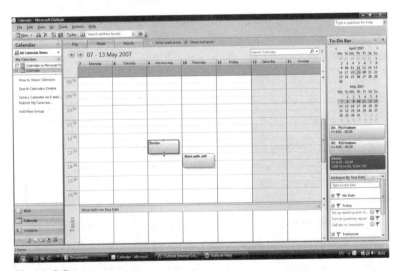

Figure 6.6

Add more time to an appointment by dragging it down.

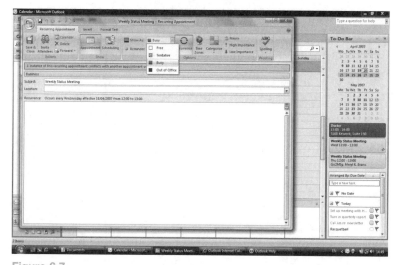

Figure 6.7
New Calendar items default to Busy, but you can change your
availability in Options.

people are Free, Tentative, Busy or Out of Office. Outlook
defaults to Busy when you create a new appointment or meeting.
However, you can still add appointments in your Calendar even if
you're free or the appointment is not final. Select the availability
status from the **Show As** dropdown in the Options group within
an appointment or meeting, as Figure 6.7 shows.

Entering an All-Day Event

Events are activities that last all day, such as birthdays,
anniversaries, travel days, holidays and other events that you want
to appear in your calendar but not at a specified time. Events don't
block out your time, as shown in Figure 6.8. To enter an Event,
click **Actions** from the menu and select **New All Day Event**. Note
that Outlook has All day event checked, so you don't have to enter
a time. Just fill in the Event, Location, dates and any notes.

Sending a Meeting Request

A meeting is an activity that includes more than one person,
occurs at a scheduled time and involves sending a meeting

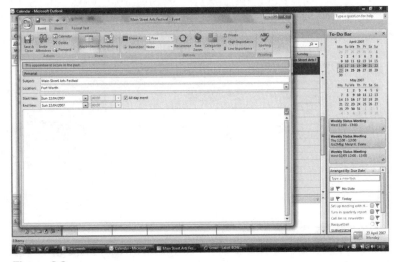

Figure 6.8

Create an all-day event.

request by e-mail, as shown in Figure 6.9. Although an appointment can involve another person, such as a doctor's appointment, you most likely can't send a meeting request to the doctor.

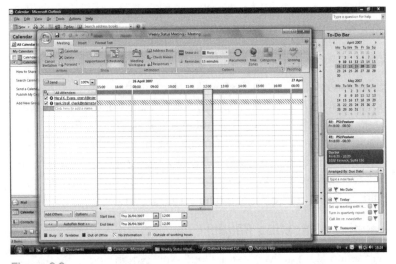

Figure 6.9

Reviewing schedules to request a meeting.

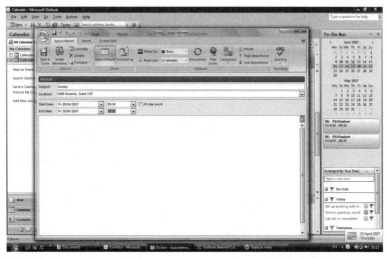

Figure 6.10
Adding an appointment in Calendar.

Meeting requests require being on an Exchange Server to take advantage of its features. You can send a meeting request to someone outside of the network, but you won't be able to check the person's schedule, as Figure 6.10 shows, or track attendees.

Unlike an appointment, a meeting on a calendar shows the location of the meeting and the meeting organiser's name, as Figure 6.11 shows. Do the following to start a meeting request:

1. Select **New** from the File menu and then choose **Meeting Request**, or use the **Ctrl+Shift+Q** shortcut.

2. Click **To** for contacts and select attendees. For optional attendees, click the contact once and click **Optional**.

3. Click **OK**.

4. Enter the subject, location and times.

5. Click **Send**.

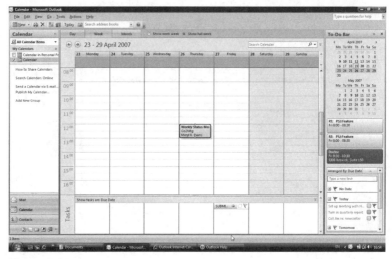

Figure 6.11
Meetings, unlike appointments, display the organiser's name.

Adding a Task

A Task is an activity that you do alone and that doesn't have a scheduled time, but you want to view it on the Calendar, as shown in Figure 6.12. You can enter a task with a start and due date. However, if you don't complete it on the schedule date, Outlook moves it to the current day and continues until you reschedule the task or mark it as complete. To add a new Task, click **New** from the File menu and then **Task**. Enter the Task name into Subject, and Select the Start and Due dates. If you want a reminder, click the box next to Reminder and select the date and time as needed. Figure 6.12 shows an example of adding a reminder to a task.

Timesaver tip

You can quickly reschedule a task in Week view by dragging the task to another date in the same week.

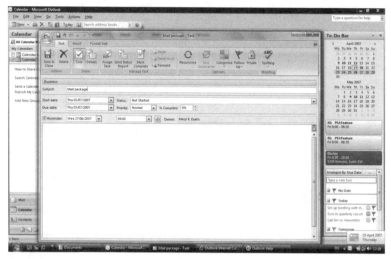

Figure 6.12

Adding a new Task.

→ Modifying and Deleting Calendar Items

Outlook lets you change the options for an appointment using the following ways:

1 **Drag and drop an item**: Move an appointment to another day, time, or both, with drag and drop.

2 **Double-click an item**: Open the item and modify the options.

3 **Right-click an item**: Open, Print, Forward, Edit Series and Delete appear in the right-click menu, as Figure 6.13 shows.

→ Creating and Modifying Recurring Calendar Items

Instead of repeatedly entering an activity that you do on a regular basis, enter it once and apply Recurrence. Recurring items may be things like exercise time, birthdays, tasks and meetings. To

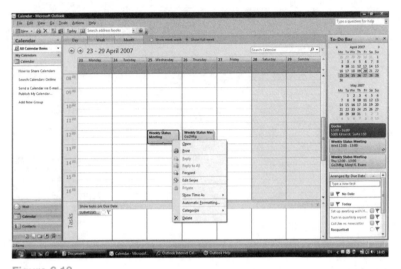

Figure 6.13

Right-click a Calendar item to modify it.

create an recurring item like the one shown in Figure 6.14, do the
following:

1 Create a new appointment, task, event or meeting by
selecting **New** from the File menu. For an event, click **All
day event** from the Appointment window.

2 Click **Recurrence**, which appears in the Options group with
a circular icon.

3 Select **Daily**, **Weekly**, **Monthly** or **Yearly** under Recurrence
pattern.

4 Select the other options as needed. Each Calendar type has
slightly different options, which are described in the
respective chapters in this book.

5 Click **OK**, and click **Save and Close**.

Timesaver tip

You can quickly identify a Calendar item as a recurring item through
its circular icon, 🔄 as Figure 6.15 shows.

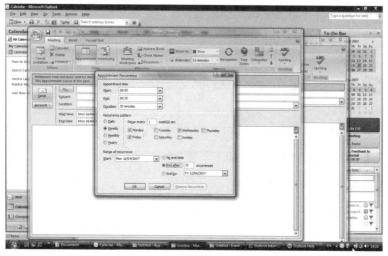

Figure 6.14

Creating a recurring appointment that occurs three times a week for ten weeks.

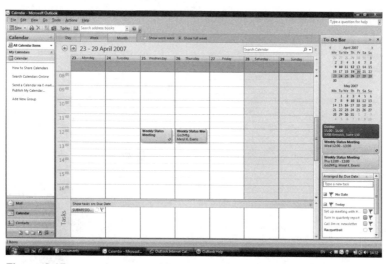

Figure 6.15

The circular icon appearing in a Calendar item indicates it's a recurring item.

Make changes to an appointment by opening the Appointment, changing its options and clicking **Save and Close**. To make changes to a recurring item's series, do the following:

1 Double-click the recurring item.

2 Select **Open the Series**, as shown in Figure 6.16 and click **OK**.

3 Change the subject, location and notes on the Recurring Appointment tab.

4 Click **Recurrence** from the Options group.

5 Change the options for the appointment, and click **OK**.

6 Click **Save and Close**.

You may need to change or delete one occurrence because of a cancellation, conflict or some other reason. The following steps show how to change one occurrence in a series:

1 Double-click the recurring item.

2 Select **Open this Occurrence**, and click **OK**.

3 Click **Delete** from the Actions group to delete this one item, or change the options on the Appointment tab.

4 Click **Save and Close**.

Figure 6.16
Select the option to edit all items in a series or one item.

Drag a Calendar item to a different date to reschedule it. If you drag a recurring item, Outlook asks whether you want to change all of the items in the series or only this occurrence. Click **Yes** for one occurrence. Changing the series requires you to open the Calendar item.

6

→ Printing from the Calendar

When printing Calendar items, you can print one appointment or print a specific view. Outlook comes with various print styles so you can print a calendar by day, week, month or year. It also allows you to set up the page and define styles. You can do a print preview of any style before printing. Print styles also include defining the font style, size, layout and custom fields. Figures 6.17–6.21 show different printing styles.

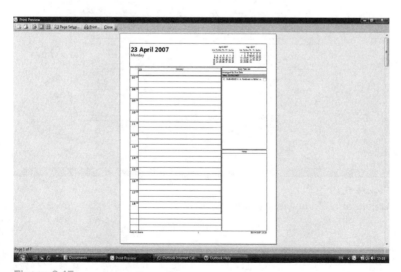

Figure 6.17
Viewing the calendar using the Daily style.

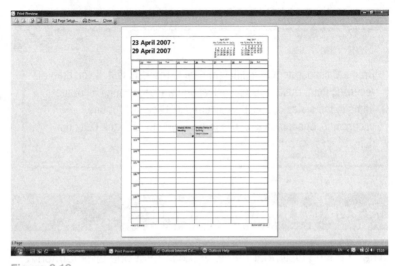

Figure 6.18
Using Weekly style to print the calendar.

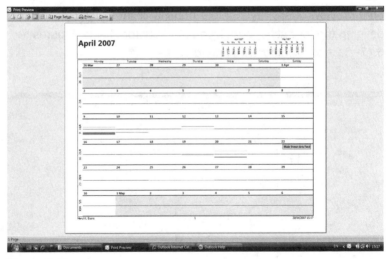

Figure 6.19
Calendar's Monthly style print preview.

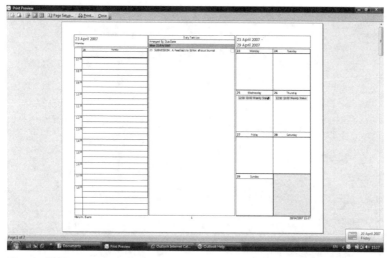

Figure 6.20

The Tri-fold style combines the current day's view, Daily Task List and Week's view.

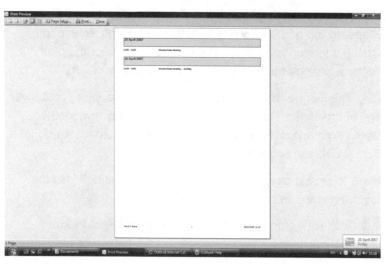

Figure 6.21

Calendar Details style provides details for the week, including dates, times and appointment subject.

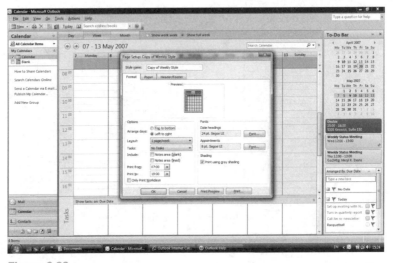

Figure 6.22

Modifying options to customise print styles.

Select a Calendar item to print it. Select the **Printer** icon from the Standard toolbar, click **Print** from the New menu, or use the **Ctrl+P** shortcut to open the Print window to select the print options, change the style or see a print preview.

Click the **Define Styles** in the Print window to copy or customise any of the styles. Options include modifying day arrangement, layout, font styles, header/footer settings and paper setup. Figure 6.22 shows the options for the Format tab.

Need to print a blank calendar to fill in at a meeting? Use the following steps to print a blank calendar:

1. Click **New** from the File menu, and then select **Folder**.

2. Enter a name for the Folder in the Create New Folder window.

3. Select **Calendar Items** from the Folder contains list.

4. Click the checkbox next to the new calendar you created in the Navigation Pane under My Calendars.

5. Click **Print** from the File menu.

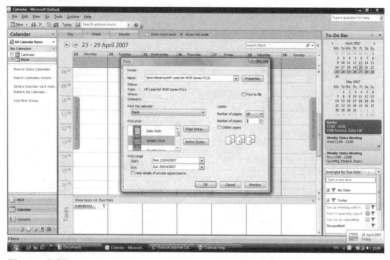

Figure 6.23
Printing a blank calendar.

6 Select the name of the new calendar under Print this calendar, as shown in Figure 6.23.

→ Sharing Calendars

Whether friends, colleagues and family members use Exchange or an application other than Outlook, they can view a Calendar item that you e-mail to them. You and others can share calendars through the Internet. Most Internet Calendars use the iCalendar format with an .ics file name extension. iCalendar makes it possible to share calendars with people who use different applications for managing calendars and e-mails.

To send a calendar by e-mail, do the following:

1 Select **Send a Calendar via E-mail** from the Navigation Pane to get the options shown in Figure 6.24.

2 Specify which calendar to send, if you have more than one.

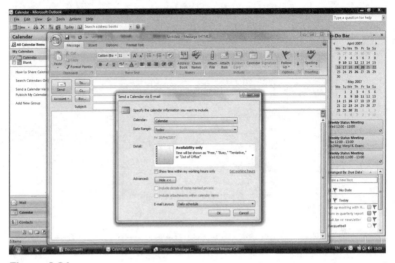

Figure 6.24

Modifying the Send a Calendar via E-mail options.

3 Select the Date Range.

4 Indicate the level of detail to show.

5 Click **Show** to view the Advanced options.

Figure 6.25

Sharing a calendar by e-mail.

Figure 6.26
Receiving the calendar in an e-mail application other than Outlook.

6 Set the remaining options, and click **OK**.

7 Enter a name or e-mail address in the To box.

8 Click **Send**.

Figure 6.25 shows what the e-mail looks like with the calendar included. Private data won't appear unless you specify otherwise, as the option appears under Advanced. Figure 6.26 shows how the calendar looks in Gmail.

Figure 6.27 shows two ways in which you can forward a Calendar item: standard for Outlook users and as an iCalendar item for people not using Outlook or if you don't know what the recipient uses.

Forward a Calendar item using the following steps:

1 Open the appointment, meeting or event.

2 Click the arrow beside Forward in the Actions group, which opens a new message.

3 Enter a name or e-mail address in the To box.

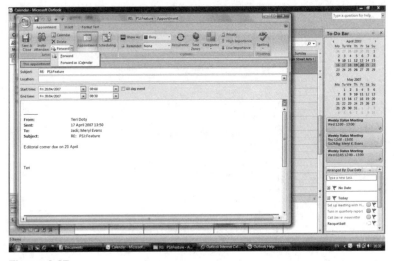

Figure 6.27

Setting the forward calendar option.

4 Modify any other options as needed.

5 Click **Send**.

Figure 6.28

Microsoft website for information on viewing and downloading
Internet Calendars.

Note the Search Calendars Online link in the Navigation Pane. Click the link to go to Microsoft's Outlook 2007 Internet Calendars website shown in Figure 6.28, where you can find and download free calendars. The website also explains how to view and subscribe to Internet calendars.

→ Working with Meeting Requests

When you receive a meeting request, you can click Calendar from the Actions group to see when the meeting occurs on your calendar. As Figure 6.29 shows, you can handle the request in one of the following ways:

■ **Accept the request**: Outlook adds the meeting to your calendar.

■ **Accept the request as tentative, stating you might come to the meeting**: Outlook adds the meeting to your calendar as tentative.

■ **Propose a new meeting time**: Outlook sends a reply to the

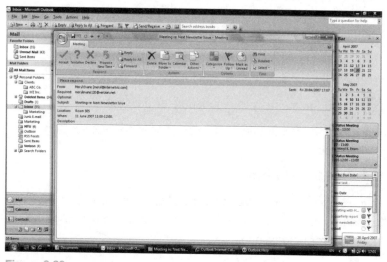

Figure 6.29
Handling a meeting request.

organiser, along with your suggested new meeting time. The calendar shows the original meeting time as tentative.

- **Decline the request**: Outlook deletes the meeting from your calendar.

After you select a response, Outlook gives you the following choices:

- Edit the response.

- Send a response.

- Don't send a response.

These choices appear whenever you act on a meeting request or change a meeting request.

You can let the meeting organiser know if you can't make a meeting that previously you agreed to attend or you need to switch to Tentative. Open the meeting and click **Decline** or another response from the Respond group in the Meeting tab. Outlook asks for a confirmation. Again, you receive an opportunity to edit, send or not send a response.

On occasion, you might not want or need to send a notification to the organiser. For example, you may need to remove a meeting notice that appears several times.

If you're the meeting organiser for a meeting that needs rescheduling or deleting, do the following:

1. Open the meeting to reschedule or delete it.

2. Change the start time and day, if needed, or click **Cancel Meeting**.

3. Click **Send Update**.

Invited attendees receive the update. Outlook updates their calendars based on their response or removes a cancelled meeting from the calendar.

→ Using Reminders

Any time you add a new item to the Calendar, by default Outlook automatically adds a reminder that notifies you 15 minutes before the start time. For events, Outlook notifies you 18 hours before they start. Change the reminder setting for a calendar item using the following steps:

1 Double-click the **Calendar** item to open it.

2 Click the down arrow next to Reminder, and select the reminder time, as Figure 6.30 shows.

3 Click the down arrow again if you wish to add sound to the reminder.

You can change the default setting for reminders from the Options menu. Go to **Options** from the Tools menu. Calendar appears under the Preferences tab. Figure 6.31 shows the options for reminders. To turn off reminders, de-select the check

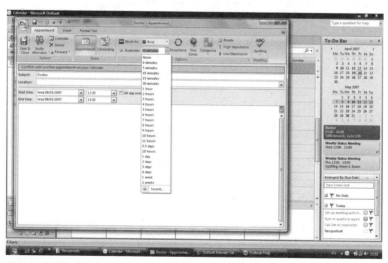

Figure 6.30

Change the reminder setting for a Calendar item.

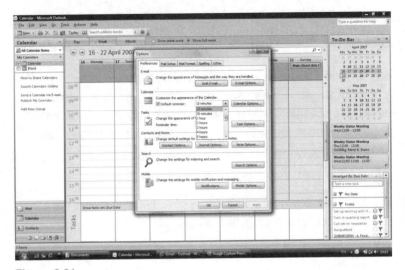

Figure 6.31
Change the default setting for reminders.

beside Default reminder. To change how much time in advance
to remind you of an appointment, select the time from the down
arrow that appears next to Calendar Options.

7

Managing Contacts

In this lesson you'll learn how to create new contacts, business cards and distribution lists.

→ Creating a New Contact and Business Card

Using Outlook's Contact module makes it easier to track and manage contacts, address e-mails simply by entering a person's name instead of typing the e-mail address, and create distribution lists for frequently e-mailed groups and teams without entering everyone's e-mail address each time you send a note to a specific group. Furthermore, people listed in your Contacts appear in your Safe Senders List so their e-mails don't filter to the junk folder.

You can either type the contact's information into a new contact form (see Figure 7.1) or let Outlook automatically fill in some of the information. Outlook also creates an Electronic Business Card for every contact. Any time you change contact information, Outlook also updates its Electronic Business Card.

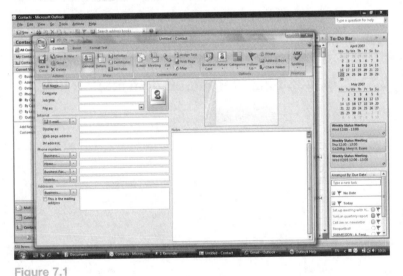

Figure 7.1

The Contact form.

You can create a new contact from within the Contact module and from an e-mail message or Electronic Business Card you receive. Create a new contact from scratch with the following steps (see Figure 7.2):

1. Switch to the Contacts module by clicking **Contacts** from the Navigation Pane.

2. Click **New** from the Standard toolbar, or use the **Ctrl+N** shortcut.

3. Fill in the form.

4. Click the photo icon next to the person's name to add a picture, if desired.

5. Click **Business Card** from the Contact tab's Options menu to edit the Electronic Business Card, and click **OK** when finished.

6. Click **Save & Close**.

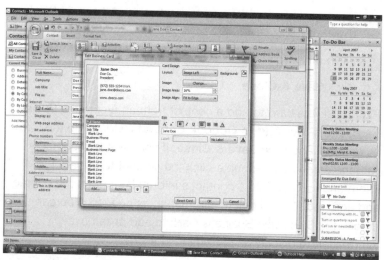

Figure 7.2
The Electronic Business Card form.

If you want to add multiple entries in a field, such as phone numbers and e-mail addresses, click the down arrow next to the field. The first listed item is the default in an item with multiple entries.

To create your own Business Card, create a Contact item with your information. If you wish to include your Business Card in every e-mail message, you can create a signature with the card, as explained in Chapter 3.

Timesaver tip

Select the down arrow next to Save & New and select **New Contact from the Same Company** to create another contact from the same company. Outlook fills in some of the same information, such as the company name, address, Web page address and phone number.

To create a new contact from an e-mail message, do the following steps:

1. Open the e-mail message from the contact you wish to add.

2. Right-click the sender's name and select **Add to Outlook Contacts**.

3. Fill in any additional fields.

4. Click **Save & Close**.

Right-click the card to add a contact from an Electronic Business Card, and select **Add to Outlook Contacts**. Complete the form as needed, and click **Save & Close**. If you have two contacts with the same name, double-click the contact to update the information. To update a contact's information, open the contact and add, modify and delete information as needed. You can modify the Electronic Business Card to add or remove information to display as shown in Figure 7.2.

→ Finding a Contact

When you need to search for a contact, you can enter a partial
name such as first name only or part of a first name if you're not
sure how to spell it. You can also search by an alias, e-mail
address, company name and other words. With Contacts open,
enter the search word(s) into the search box where it says
Search Contacts at the top of the Contacts page (see
Figure 7.3).

Click a letter from the alphabet column displayed on the right-
hand side of the cards to find contacts from Business Cards,
Address Cards and Detailed Address Cards views, as Figure 7.4
shows.

You can change the contact sorting and viewing from any of the
tables views such as Phone List, By Category and Outlook Data
Files. Click any of the column headers to change the sorting from
ascending to descending, and vice versa. If you have multiple
items in a Category, Company or Location sort, you can click

Figure 7.3
Quickly search Contacts using its search box.

Figure 7.4
Click a letter from the index to find Contacts.

another column to sort those items. Figure 7.5 shows two entries
for the same company with Full Name selected to sort names in
descending order (A–Z).

Figure 7.5
Click the header to change the sort column and sort order.

You can search for a contact from other Outlook modules by clicking the **Address Book** icon ▣.

→ Forwarding a Contact

Whether the recipient uses Outlook 2007 or an older version, you can forward a contact to share. Outlook 2007 users will receive the contact as an Electronic Business Card. People using an older version of Outlook or e-mail applications that rely on HTML see the contact information as an image that looks like the Electronic Business Card and a .vcf file attachment, as shown in Figure 7.6. Other users, especially those receiving e-mail messages in plain text, will receive a contact's information as a .vcf file attachment.

From within an e-mail message, click the **Business Card** icon in the Message tab's Include Group. Select the default business card or **Other Business Cards** to find a different contact from the Insert Business Card window. The window includes Business

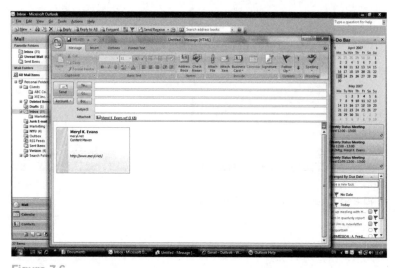

Figure 7.6
Forward contact information through an e-mail message.

Card Preview, as Figure 7.7 shows, so you can confirm you have the right card, since you may have multiple entries for one person.

You can also send a Business Card from the Contacts module. Open a Contact you wish to send and click **Send** to receive a menu. Select the format you wish to send. This creates a new e-mail message, where you enter the recipient and any other information to send the message.

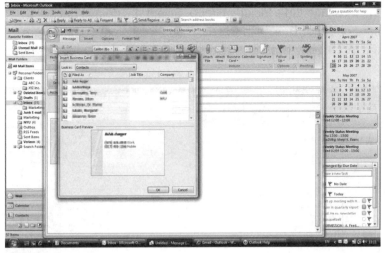

Figure 7.7

Find and insert a Business Card into an e-mail message.

→ Creating Distribution Lists

If you regularly send e-mail messages to a committee, a team or family members, a distribution list can save you time in entering e-mail addresses each time you send them a message. A distribution list contains a group of Contacts with its own name. You might create lists called Event Committee, Team and Family. You can also use distribution lists in task requests and meeting requests, if you have Exchange. Create a distribution list like the one shown in Figure 7.8 with the following steps:

1 Click **New** from the File menu, and select **Distribution List**, or use **Ctrl+Shift+L** shortcut.

2 Enter a name in the Name box.

3 Click **Select Members** from the Distribution List tab's Members group for those listed in Contacts.

4 Select the Address Book by clicking the down arrow under Address book.

Figure 7.8
Create a distribution list to quickly send messages to groups.

5 Enter the name into the search box to quickly navigate the list, select the name and click **Members**.

6 Repeat Step 5 for each member you want in the distribution list, and click **OK** when finished.

7 Click **Add New** from the Distribution List tab's Members group to add members who don't appear in Contacts.

8 Complete the Add New Member form as shown in Figure 7.9, and click **OK**.

9 Click **Save & Close**.

To send a message to the newly created distribution list, open a new e-mail message and enter the name of the list into the **To** box. You can click **To** and open the Contact list to search for the name of the distribution list. Complete the e-mail message and send it.

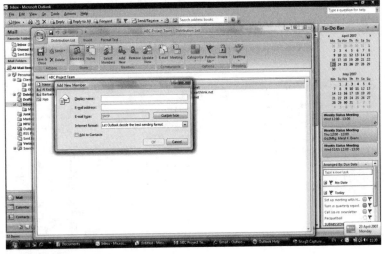

Figure 7.9

Add a new member who doesn't appear in Contacts to the distribution list.

To add or delete names from a distribution list, click the **Address Book** icon and locate the distribution list. Double-click the list to manage the list. Click **Remove** to delete a name. Once done, click **Save & Close**.

→ Creating another Address Book

Why would you want more than one address book when you can group people in distribution lists? You might want separate address books for business and personal use. Outlook 2007 adds a Mobile Address Book.

People on an Exchange Server have a Global Address List that has the names and addresses of everyone in the organisation. Adding an Outlook Address Book outside the Global Address List allows you to add people who aren't in the organisation or on the same Exchange Server. Create an additional Address Book with the following steps:

1 Click **Account Settings** in the Tools menu.

2 Select the **Address Book** tab and click **New**, as shown in Figure 7.10.

3 Select **Additional Address Books**, and click **Next**.

4 Select the address book you want to create (Mobile Address Book or Outlook Address Book), and click **Next**.

5 Exit and start Outlook to start using the new address book.

Jargon buster

Lightweight Directory Access Protocol (LDAP), also known as Internet directory services, lets you add contacts into Outlook from an Internet-based directory. For example, some colleges and universities have LDAP directories so that students and staff can access contact information using LDAP.

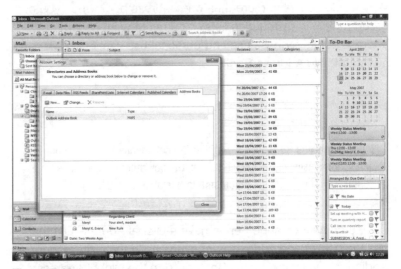

Figure 7.10

Create a new Address Book.

Create an Internet address book (LDAP) using the following steps:

1 Click **Account Settings** in the Tools menu.

2 Select the **Address Book** tab, and click **New**.

3 Select **Internet Directory Service (LDAP)**, and click **Next**.

4 Enter the server information you received from your Internet service provider or system administrator. You may need to click **More Settings**, as shown in Figure 7.11.

5 Click **Next**, and then exit and start Outlook to start using the new address book.

Important

Personal Address Books (.pab) can't be created or used with Outlook 2007. You can still import and convert old .pab files as Contacts into Outlook 2007.

Remove an address book using the following steps:

1 Click **Account Settings** from the Tools menu.

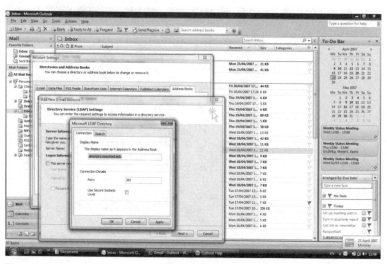

Figure 7.11
Modify the settings to connect to an LDAP directory.

2 Select the **Address Book** tab, and select the Address Book to remove.

3 Click **Remove**, and then click **Yes**.

→ Printing Contact Information

Outlook lets you print one contact, some contacts or all contacts. You can also select the fields you want to print. To print names and selected fields, do the following:

1 Select **Address Cards** or **Phone List** (the latter prints in a table format as Figure 7.12 shows, while the former has various styles) from the Contacts Navigation Pane.

2 Click **Customize Current View** in the Navigation Pane.

3 Click **Fields** to open the Show Fields window, as shown in Figure 7.13.

4 Select items from the Available fields column, and click **Add** to include them.

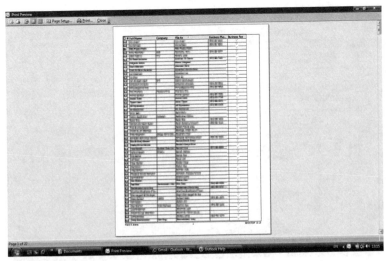

Figure 7.12
Print Contacts in a table format.

5 Select items from the Show these fields in this order column, and click **Remove** to take them out.

6 Select a field in the right-hand column to move it up or down to change the order in which the fields appear.

7 Click **OK** to exit the Show Fields window.

8 Select **Print** from the File menu.

9 Select the Print Style, and click **OK** to print, or click **Preview** to view before printing.

If you want to return the view back to default, click **Customize Current View in the Navigation Pane** and **Reset Current View**.

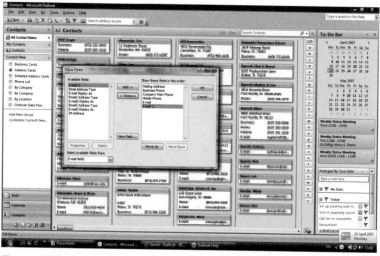

Figure 7.13
Select and remove fields to appear in print.

Managing Notes

In this lesson you'll learn how to create, manage, forward and delete Notes. You'll also learn about using Journal.

Sticking notes all around your monitor and desk? Clear the clutter and use Outlook's Notes feature. Using Outlook's Notes instead of sticky notes protects your information since it's stored on your computer instead of out in the open for all to see. You can even categorise, print and organise these electronic notes.

Open the notes from anywhere in Outlook by clicking the yellow sticky note icon at the bottom of the Navigation Pane, as Figure 8.1 shows.

When you have Notes open, you can click **New** in the Standard toolbar to create a new note, just as with any other item in Outlook. Use the **Ctrl+Shift+N** shortcut to create a Note from any place in Outlook. Start typing a Note and Outlook automatically saves it, even if it stays open while you do other tasks. Outlook also saves when you click **X** to close the Note.

The first line of the Note becomes the title for the Note for easier finding within the Notes list, as Figure 8.2 shows. But if you don't

Figure 8.1

Accessing Notes in Outlook.

Figure 8.2

The first line of the Note becomes the title in the Notes list.

want the entire first sentence to appear, hit **Enter** at the cut-off point, as shown in Figure 8.3.

Notice the bottom of the note displays the date and time you created the Note. Close the note, wait a few minutes and open it

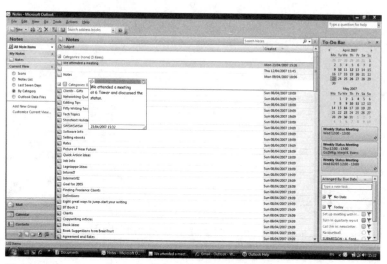

Figure 8.3

Press the Enter key to shorten the Note's title.

again to see that the time has not changed. The date and time reflect the Note's last edit.

Timesaver tip

Enter a URL as a hyperlink, and Notes makes the link clickable. Just enter *www.address.com* without the *http* and Outlook instantly creates a clickable link.

→ Managing Notes

Click once on the **Note** icon that appears in the upper left corner to see a menu, as Figure 8.4 shows. With this menu, you have all the options for managing Notes including the following:

■ Create a new Note.

■ Use Save As to save the Note in another format such as Rich

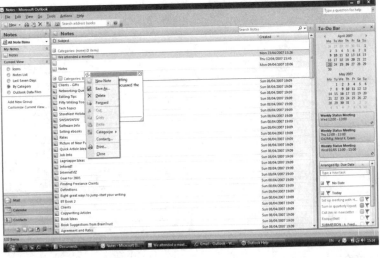

Figure 8.4
Opening the Notes menu.

Figure 8.5

Saving the Note in another file format.

Text Format, Text Only or Outlook Message Format, as Figure 8.5 shows.

■ Delete the Note.

■ Forward the Note.

■ Cut, copy and paste selected text from the Note.

■ Categorise the Note.

■ Associate the Note with Contacts.

■ Print the Note.

■ Close the Note (although clicking **X** is faster).

Outlook provides other ways to manage and organise Notes, but this menu contains all the items in one place. To edit a note, double-click the Note while you're in the Notes folder to open and edit it.

Changing Notes Views

The Icons view is the default view where Notes appear on the screen along with their titles as shown in Figure 8.1. As with

Figure 8.6

Viewing notes edited in the past seven days.

other Outlook folders, change the view by selecting a different view in the Navigation Panel with the Notes folder open.

Figure 8.6 shows the Last Seven Days view, which displays Notes edited within the past seven days. Select the different views to see how Notes appear.

Deleting Notes

Rather than using the menu that appears by clicking on the Notes icon, you can select a Note and press **Delete**. To delete more than one Note at a time, hold down the **Ctrl** key to select the Notes and click **Delete**.

Forwarding Notes

You can send one or multiple Notes to someone else using Forward. Select one note or use **Ctrl** to select multiple notes. Then right-click an item and select **Forward Items** from the menu. Figure 8.7 shows the selected notes to forward.

Figure 8.8 shows the Notes in an e-mail message ready for addressing. Complete the e-mail message and click **Send**.

Figure 8.7

Forwarding multiple Notes.

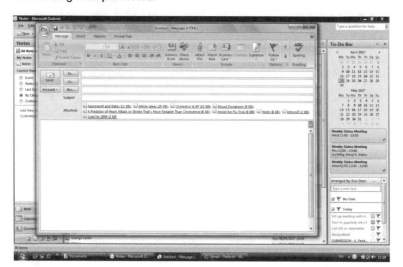

Figure 8.8

Addressing an e-mail message with Notes for forwarding.

Important

People who don't use Outlook will most likely not be able to open and view Notes. In this case, copying and pasting the note into a blank e-mail message would work better.

Editing Notes

You can cut, copy and paste Notes into other documents, e-mail messages and other applications. To cut or copy text, select the text in the Note. After highlighting the text to cut or copy, right-click the highlighted text and click **Cut or Copy**. Open the document or application where you want to paste the content and press **Ctrl+V**, or find the **Paste** command.

Categorising Notes

The easiest way to categorise a Note is to right-click it, select **Categorize** and pick the category, as shown in Figure 8.9. If you accidentally select the wrong category or want to remove a category, pick the category again and Outlook will de-select the category.

Figure 8.9

Categorising a Note.

When you categorise a Note, the Note receives the colour of its category. Any Note without a category receives the colour selected in the Notes Options. The default colour is yellow. Change the default colour, size and font by doing the following:

Carte postale = 178 € ttc

Carte de visite = 107 € ttc

affiche A3 = 380 € ttc

500 ex.

1. Click **Options** from the Tools menu.

2. Click **Note Options**, as shown in Figure 8.10.

3. Click the down arrow next to **Color and Size** to change each option.

4. Click **Font** to open Font options and change the font, font style, size, effects and colour, and then click **OK**.

5. Click **OK** twice to exit Options.

Figure 8.10
Accessing Notes options.

Existing Notes won't change colour, even if they're the previous default colour. New Notes, however, reflect the new colour you selected from the Notes Options, as shown in Figure 8.11.

Associating Notes with Contacts

Outlook 2007 improves how its applications interact with one another to become a complete personal information manager rather than one with five different applications doing their own thing. You can associate Notes with Contacts and the Notes appear on the Contacts' Activities page. The following steps associate a Note with Contacts:

Figure 8.11

Modifying default Notes options.

1 Click the **Notes** icon in the Note, and select **Contacts**.

2 Click **Contacts** to select Contacts to associate with the
Note. To select more than one Contact, select a name and

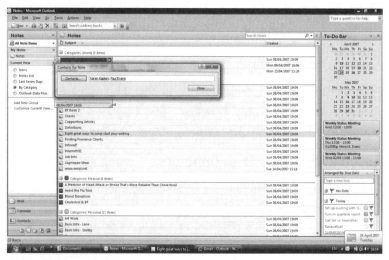

Figure 8.12

Verifying the Contacts associated with the Note.

click **Apply**. Repeat for each name, and click **OK** when finished.

3 Verify that the right names appear in the Contacts for Note window, as Figure 8.12 shows. To delete a name from the list, select it and click **Delete**.

4 Click **Close**.

To see the Contact's association with the Note, do the following:

1 Open the Contacts folder.

2 Open the contact's card.

3 Click **Activities** from the Show group on the Contact tab.

Printing Notes

Just as you can print one, some or all of your Contacts, so you can do the same with Notes. In printing Notes, Outlook puts each one on its own page. This can waste paper, especially with short Notes.

Outlook prints all of a Note's information, including the modified time and date, categories, contacts and the body of the Note.

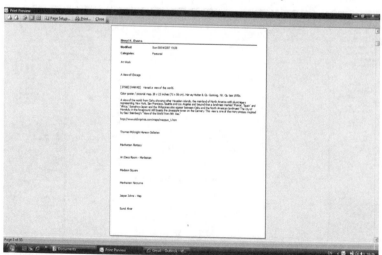

Figure 8.13
Previewing a Note before printing.

The Note in Figure 8.13 contains headers for Modified and Categories. Since it doesn't have Contacts associated with it, Outlook omits the line.

→ Using Journal

Journal tracks e-mail messages associated with a contact and Microsoft Office documents, but the Activities page for a contact also provides this information. People who want to track documents will probably benefit most from Journal. For tracking contacts and e-mails, Activities is the better choice, since it requires no action from you.

Journal tracks your time spent on Microsoft Office documents, including Microsoft Access, Microsoft Excel, Microsoft PowerPoint, Microsoft Project, Microsoft Visio and Microsoft Word.

Outlook can automatically record activities with these documents and display them in a timeline. Open Journal to view Journal

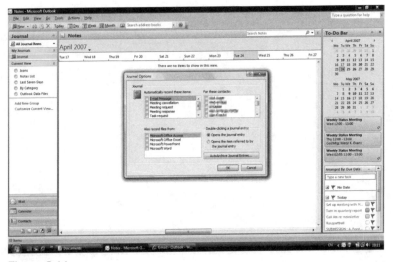

Figure 8.14

Setting up automatic recording with Journal.

Figure 8.15
Adding Journal to the Navigation Pane.

Options, as Figure 8.14 shows. Journal, however, doesn't appear in the Navigation Pane. You can add the Journal icon to appear at the bottom of the pane along with Tasks, Notes, Folder List and Shortcuts. To add Journal, click the down arrow on the bottom of the Navigation Pane and select **Navigation Pane Options**, as shown in Figure 8.15. Click the **Journal** icon to receive a message to turn on the Journal. Click **Yes** to get to the Journal Options window, where you can set up a recording.

Note that Journal Options lists Microsoft applications loaded on the computer. The Activities page for a Contact does the same thing that Automatically record these items does without setting up anything. To use Journal to track e-mail, Notes, tasks, documents and other activities, do the following steps:

1. Click **Options** on the Tools menu.

2. Click **Journal Options** on the Preferences tab.

3. Select the items you want to automatically record.

4. Select the contacts that you want Journal to record.

Figure 8.16

Viewing Journal details.

5 Select the files that you want to record.

6 Click **OK** twice to exit the Options windows.

Figure 8.17

Viewing Journal entries by type and date.

Figure 8.16 shows activities including the entry type, file location, start and duration. Figure 8.17 shows the activities by type and by date.

> ## Timesaver tip
>
> Rather than opening a document that Journal tracks through the document's application, open it through Journal. Open the Journal entry and click the file. If you want to keep a document open when you're not working on it, click **Start Timer** or **Pause Timer** to manage time tracking, as Figure 8.18 shows.

If you accidentally keep the timer running longer than the actual activity, you can change the duration. Open the Journal entry, select the number, and type in the new number in the Duration box. Click the arrow next to Duration for a list of common duration options ranging from ten minutes to two weeks.

Journal views work like any Outlook tool. Change the view by selecting the view from the Navigation Pane. You can add new

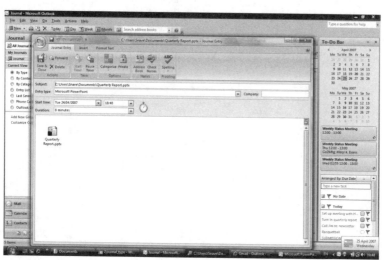

Figure 8.18

Tracking the time spent on a Journal-tracked document.

groups and customise views. Select a Journal item to assign categories and click **Categorize** from the Action menu to choose the category. Repeat the step to add another category.

You can't associate a Journal item with a contact from within Journal's folder, but you can do it from the Contacts folder using the following steps:

1 Click **Contacts** and select a contact without opening it.

2 Select **Create** from the Actions menu, and click **New Journal Entry** for Contact.

3 Select the Entry type.

4 Switch to the Insert tab and click **Attach Item** to attach an existing Journal item, as Figure 8.19 shows.

5 Click the **Journal** folder from the Insert Item list, and select the item from the Items list.

6 Select the option of how you want the file inserted from the Insert as list, and click **OK**.

7 Click **Save & Close** from the Journal Entry tab.

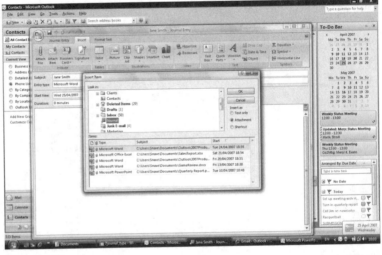

Figure 8.19

Associating a Journal item with a contact.

Figure 8.20

Searching Journal entries.

You can create any kind of Journal entry and attach files even if they don't exist in Journal. Use the Journal Entry tabs to insert files, tables, illustrations and more as well as to start and stop the timer.

Figure 8.21

Viewing the results of a Journal search.

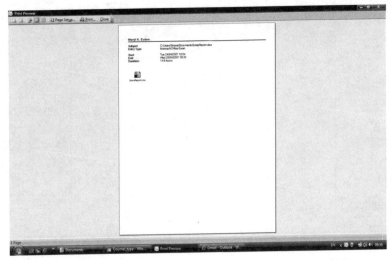

Figure 8.22
Previewing Journal before printing.

Use the search box from within Journal's folder to search Journal entries, as Figure 8.20 shows. Figure 8.21 shows the results from a keyword search.

Printed Journal entries resemble a printed e-mail message. They include headers indicating the file name, document type and times, as Figure 8.22 shows.

Select the Journal item and click **Print** from the File menu to print.

Using RSS Feeds

In this lesson you'll get an introduction to Really Simple Syndication (RSS), discover how to find, add, read, forward, share and manage feeds.

Really Simple Syndication (RSS) provides a standard format that gives users a way to access content from blogs, podcasts, websites and any other resource that contains an RSS feed. RSS feeds allow publishers to publish content in one format that many applications known as RSS aggregators, feed readers and news readers can read and view. Feeds also make it possible for users to access their content in one place instead of hopping from website to website to get the information.

Jargon buster

RSS stands for Really Simple Syndication and Rich Site Summary. It gives publishers a standard format to deliver frequently updated content as an XML file. Users copy the link pointing to the XML file into a feed reader or feed aggregator application. The feed reader presents the information in a readable format. Users who rely on feed readers can receive updated content from websites, blogs and other resources in one place.

Outlook can accept and read RSS feeds. Although Outlook is more than an RSS reader, it offers the same features and functionality that you find in a standard RSS reader. If it weren't for feed reader applications such as Outlook, RSS feeds would look garbled, as Figure 9.1 shows.

Jargon buster

XML (eXtensible Markup Language) is a general markup language for sharing information across different platforms and applications.

Figure 9.1

Viewing an RSS file without an application.

Figure 9.2

Many sites use the orange button with radio waves icon to indicate an RSS feed.

Many sites indicate they have a feed with a square orange RSS icon with radio waves, as Figure 9.2 shows, but many variations exist, as shown in Figure 9.3.

You can think of RSS feeds as another way for publishers to deliver content and for users to receive content. Websites, e-mail messages and newsletters also deliver content. For example, you

Figure 9.3
Figure 9.3
Other variations indicating an RSS feed on a website.

may get your local news from your city's newspaper. You could get the same content in print, on the newspaper's website, through a feed that you read in an application, through an audio feed that you listen to with an MP3 player, through a video feed that you view on your computer or handheld device that can handle video files, in an e-mail message or in an e-mail newsletter.

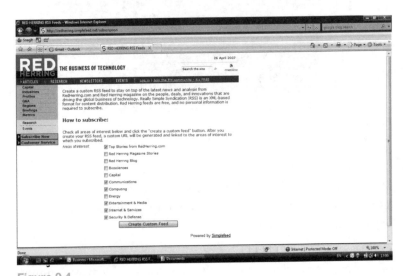

Figure 9.4
Customising a feed.

Figure 9.5

Viewing a feed's link in Internet Explorer's address bar.

Maybe you only want to read the sports and business sections. Some websites make it possible to customise feeds so you get only the feeds you want, or they offer multiple feeds. Red Herring, shown in Figure 9.4, lets you customise a feed by selecting your areas of interest. All you need is the URL of the feed to begin using it.

For most feeds, you can click the feed link to get the URL from the browser's address bar, as Figure 9.5 shows.

Copy that URL and paste it in to any RSS feed reader or directly into Outlook. Most feeder URLs end with an .xml extension, but some don't.

Important

Because of Outlook's synchronising with Internet Explorer 7 feeds, the process can slow Outlook's performance. You can disable RSS Sync and remove all the feeds to improve performance.

To disable RSS Sync, do the following:

1 Click **Options** in the Tools menu.

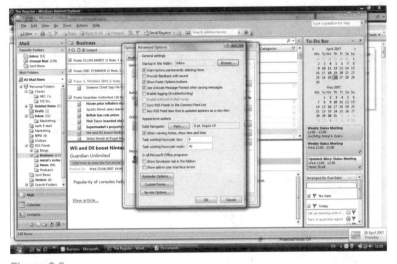

Figure 9.6

Disabling RSS Sync.

2 Select the **Other** tab and click **Advanced Options**.

3 Uncheck Sync RSS Feeds to the Common Feed List, as Figure 9.6 shows, and click **OK**.

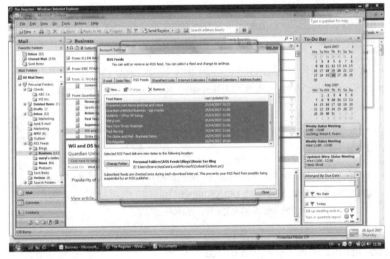

Figure 9.7

Removing all subscribed feeds.

4 Click the **Mail Setup** tab and click **Data Files**.

5 Click the **RSS Feeds** tab.

6 Click the first feed.

7 Press **Shift** and **PgDn** until all feeds appear highlighted, as Figure 9.7 shows.

8 Click **Remove**, and click **Yes** to confirm deleting all the feeds.

→ Finding and Adding Feeds

If you see a feed icon on a website, you can subscribe to the feed with Outlook. You can also find feeds in feeds directories such as 2RSS.com and Syndic8 (see Figures 9.8 and 9.9), which are websites containing hundreds or thousands of feeds that you can search.

You can also share feeds with others by e-mail and sharing files with an .opml extension. OPML files contain many RSS feeds for easy importing and exporting.

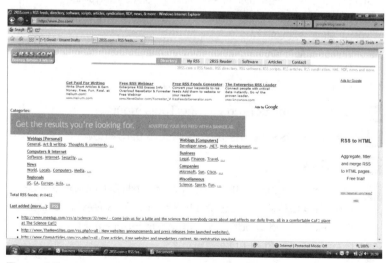

Figure 9.8
Searching for RSS feeds in 2RSS.com.

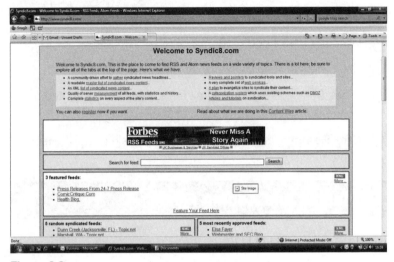

Figure 9.9

Using Syndic8.com to find RSS feeds.

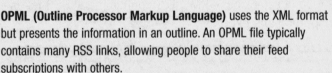
To add a feed in Outlook, do the following:

1 Click **Account Settings** on the Tools menu.

2 Select the **RSS Feeds** tab, as Figure 9.10 shows.

3 Click **New**.

4 Select and highlight the URL, press **Ctrl+C** to copy the URL, and use **Ctrl+V** to paste the link to the RSS feed into the New RSS Feed window, as shown in Figure 9.11.

5 Click **OK** to open the RSS Feed Options window, as Figure 9.12 shows.

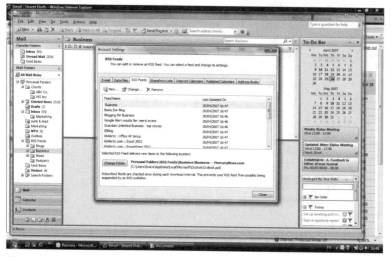

Figure 9.10

Add, change and remove feeds in the Account Settings RSS Feeds tab.

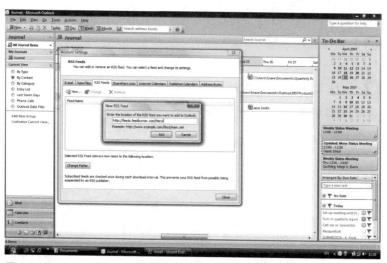

Figure 9.11

Pasting the URL of a new feed.

6 Change the name of the feed, if needed.

7 Click **Change Folder**, if you want the feed saved in a different folder as Figure 9.13 shows. Click **New Folder** to

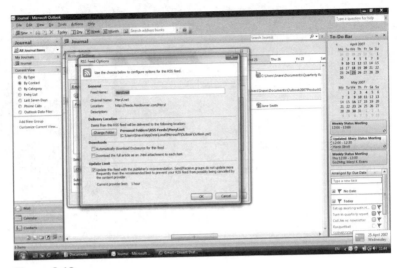

Figure 9.12

Modifying RSS feed options for the new feed.

create a subfolder under RSS Feeds or the currently selected folder to organise your feeds. Click **OK**.

8 Leave the update limit box checked (see the Important note on the next page).

9 Click **Close** to exit Account Settings.

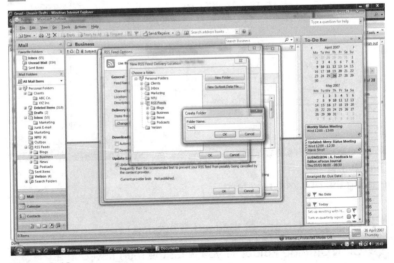

Figure 9.13

Creating a new folder for the feed.

Important

If you check for updates on a feed too frequently, the publisher may suspend your RSS feed subscription. The length of the suspension depends on the publisher, and Outlook has no control over the suspension. You can view the publisher's update limit in the RSS Feed Options window. Click **Account Settings** from the Tools menu, switch to the **RSS Feeds** tab, select the feed you want to view and click **Change**. The limit appears on the bottom of the window.

If you have an OPML file, you can download many RSS feeds at the same time. A friend could export feeds from a feed reader as an OPML file and you can import them into Outlook. Importing and exporting feeds as an OPML file simplifies sharing and moving feeds between applications. Import an OPML file using the following steps:

1 Select **Import and Export** from the File menu to open the Import and Export Wizard.

2 Select **Import RSS Feeds from an OPML file**, as Figure 9.14 shows, and click **Next**.

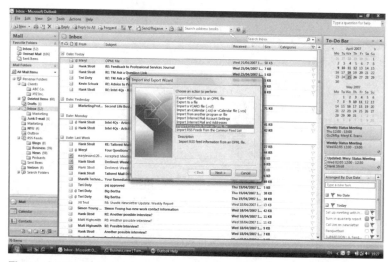

Figure 9.14

Using the Import Wizard to import an OPML file, and click Next.

Figure 9.15
Opening the OPML file.

3 Click **Browse** to locate the OPML file, as Figure 9.15 shows.

4 Click **Open** and **Next**.

5 Select the feeds you want to import, or click **Select All**

Figure 9.16
Selecting the feeds to import.

to import all feeds, as shown in Figure 9.16, and click **Next**.

6 Click **Finish**.

The drawback of using this method is that each feed receives its own folder. This could create a long list of folders under the RSS Feed folder. You can drag the feed folder into another folder. For more on managing folders, see later in this chapter.

Outlook comes with feeds to help you get started. Access them by clicking on the **RSS Feeds** or **RSS Subscriptions** folder, as Figure 9.17 shows. Click any item and Outlook asks whether you want to add the RSS Feed. Click **Yes** to automatically add it, or click **Advanced** to modify the feed's settings before adding the feed. Remember you can always change the feed's settings from the RSS Feeds tab in Account Settings.

Automatically download Enclosures for this feed in RSS Feed Options means including any attachments that appear in the RSS feed. Outlook does not download attachments by default. To change this, do the following:

1 Click **Account Settings** on the Tools menu.

2 Select the **RSS Feeds** tab.

3 Select the feed you want to change, and click **Change**.

4 Select the checkbox next to Automatically download Enclosures for this feed, and click **OK**.

5 Close **Account Settings**.

In the same way with e-mail messages having attachments, Outlook lets you know an item has an attachment by showing a paperclip icon next to the feed entry.

Important

Attachments with feeds can have potentially unsafe files. Use an antivirus application to check such attachments.

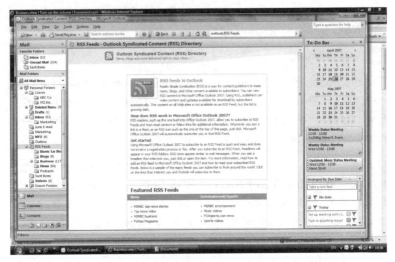

Figure 9.17

Subscribing to feeds included in Outlook's RSS folder.

The other download option includes the article as an attachment instead of as a link. When using the Download linked article as an attachment option, the feed contains the HTML file as an attachment similar to an e-mail message with an attachment.

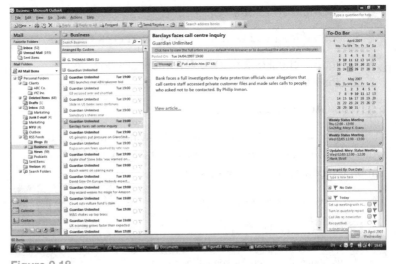

Figure 9.18

Viewing an item that contains an attached article.

Figure 9.18 shows an article from a feed with the attachment and link. This makes it possible to read feeds while offline and to save the article on your computer.

To change the option to view articles as HTML attachments, do the following:

1 Click **Account Settings** on the Tools menu.

2 Select the **RSS Feeds** tab.

3 Select the feed you want to change, and click **Change**.

4 Select the checkbox next to Download the full article as an .html attachment to each item, and click **OK**.

5 Close **Account Settings**.

You can also preview the attachment. Click the attachment once to select it and click **Preview file**, as Figure 9.19 shows. Notice the images don't appear. Outlook blocks images as a security precaution. Click the Infobar to view the pictures.

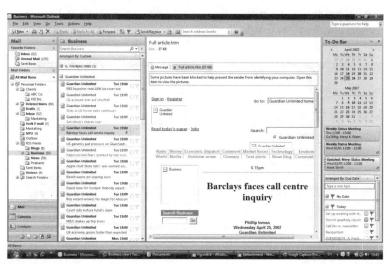

Figure 9.19
Previewing an attached article.

→ Reading Feeds

Feeds appear in Outlook's RSS Feeds folder as subfolders. Each
subfolder represents a feed and contains articles or items from
that feed. Each article is a message like an e-mail message. The
Reading Pane works in the same way for feeds as for e-mail
messages. Scan the items and click the one you want to read.
The article should appear in the Preview window unless you have
the Reading Pane turned off. You can also double-click the item
to see it in its own window.

Figure 9.20

Viewing an article using the Bottom Reading Pane view.

Click Reading Pane from the View menu to select the view for the current view. Figure 9.20 shows the Bottom view. A typical item contains a short summary followed by a link to "View article." Click the link to read the full article in the browser.

If you don't download articles as attachments by default, you can do so on an individual item basis. Click the Infobar above the Posted On field to choose to view the full article in the browser or download the content, as Figure 9.21 shows. Keeping the download article to a minimum avoids using space on your hard disk.

Another way to download content is through an open article window. Click the **Download Content** icon from the Actions group, and select **Download article**.

Feeds can be sorted using the Arrange By menu on the View menu. You can change the sort by clicking the header of the item you want to sort by. Click the header again to reverse the sorting. To group items, do the following:

1 Click **Current View** from the View menu, and select **Customize Current View**.

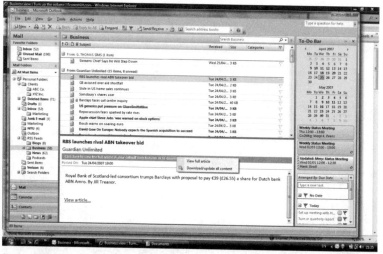

Figure 9.21
Clicking the Infobar to view or download the full article.

Figure 9.22

Showing Group By field in every item.

2 Click **Group By** and uncheck the box next to Automatically group according to arrangement.

3 Select a field from the Group items by dropdown list, and select more fields for sorting, if needed.

Figure 9.23

Showing Group By field for groups only.

4 Select another field, if needed, from the **Then by** dropdown list.

The Show field in view in Group By states whether to display the field for every item or to leave it off. Figure 9.22 shows the From field in view for every item, whereas Figure 9.23 does not.

After you read an item and select another, Outlook marks the item as read. Double-clicking an item does the same thing.

AutoPreview on the View menu provides a summary of each item, as Figure 9.24 shows.

If the Reading Pane is off, double-click any item to open it.

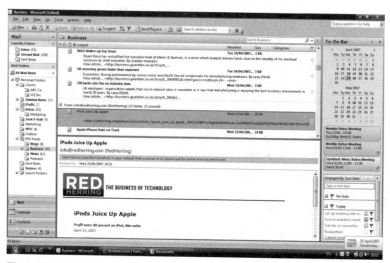

Figure 9.24
AutoPreview displays the first three lines of each item.

Figure 9.25
Outlook adds new feeds in their own folders by default.

→ Managing Feeds

Subscribing to a handful of feeds can easily lead to you receiving over 100 items a day. Getting hundreds of messages in one sitting overwhelms many people. Outlook offers flexibility to help you manage feeds. When adding a new feed, Outlook gives the feed its own folder. Click the + next to the RSS folder to expand its list. Figure 9.25 shows Meryl's notes blog in its own folder after adding the feed. It also shows folders with generic names for putting multiple feeds of the same category. For example, the News folder contains feeds from news sites.

Organising Feeds

Every one has different preferences for managing e-mail and messages. However, the following lists the possibilities on what you can do to organise feeds.

■ Right-click a folder to rename it, move it, delete it or create a new folder under it, as Figure 9.26 shows.

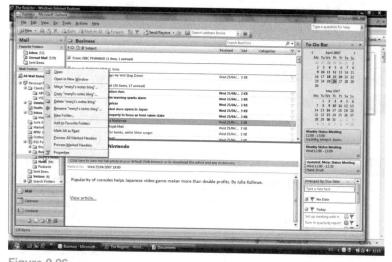

Figure 9.26

Reviewing options for managing a message.

- Click and drag a folder to move it into another folder or out of a folder.

- Create folders for categories and put feeds under the appropriate category.

- Create folders for feeds to read daily, monthly, weekly and occasionally, and move the feeds into the appropriate folder.

- Go into the **RSS** tab of the Account Settings, select a feed and click **Change Folder** to change the folder or create a new folder for the feed.

- File individual items into your folders outside the RSS folder if they're worth keeping or referring to later. Remember flagging works with RSS feeds.

Searching Feeds

You may need to find an article covering a specific topic. Rather than scanning every relevant feed and its items, use the Search tool at the top of Outlook's window. If you have a feed's folder selected, search tool will limit its search to that folder. However, if you want to search all of the folders in RSS Feed or RSS Subscriptions, do the following:

1 Select the **RSS Folder**.

2 Press **Ctrl+Shift+F** to open the Advanced Find window, which already has search the RSS Feed folder selected.

3 Click the arrow next to the Look for field and select **Any type of Outlook item**. Skipping this step limits the search to only items in the RSS folder. The search tool won't look in the subfolders.

4 Enter the word(s) to search.

5 Click the arrow in the In field to select the subject field and message body, as shown in Figure 9.27.

6 Complete any other fields if needed, and click **Find Now** to begin searching.

Figure 9.27
Searching for a word in the entire RSS Feeds folder.

Deleting Feeds

Deleting feeds and feed items on a regular schedule helps keep Outlook lean and manageable. Those feeds can grow out of control like weeds. You may also find you don't need some subscriptions any more. Remove RSS Feeds by doing the following steps:

1 Click **Account Settings** in the Tools menu.

2 Click the **Mail Setup** tab, and click **Data Files**.

3 Click the **RSS Feeds** tab.

4 Choose the feed to delete, and click **Remove**.

5 Click **Yes** to confirm you want to delete the feed.

If you have feeds in their own folders, just select the folder and press **Delete** to remove the feed from Outlook for good.

Timesaver tip

To delete more than one feed from the RSS Feeds window, hold down **Ctrl** and click each feed to delete. After selecting all the feeds to delete, click **Remove**. You can also press **Ctrl** and click each feed folder and press **Delete**.

Delete individual items using any of the following ways:

■ Press **Delete** when you want to delete an open or currently selected article.

■ Right-click the selected item(s) and select **Delete** from the menu, as Figure 9.28 shows.

■ Press **Ctrl+A** to select all the items currently shown, and press **Delete** to delete all of the selected items.

■ Right-click the **Group By** item and select **Delete** to delete all of the articles in that group, as Figure 9.29 shows.

Figure 9.28

Deleting all items in a folder using Delete on the right-click menu.

Figure 9.29

Delete all the articles under a Group By item.

→ Forwarding and Sharing Feeds

By now you know that feed items behave similarly to e-mail messages. This includes forwarding, flagging, printing, moving and deleting items. One thing you can't do with feeds, however, is reply or leave a comment in blog discussions from within the feed.

Forwarding a feed creates a new e-mail message containing the article's headers, short summary and link to the article as shown in Figure 9.30. Right-click the item to forward it, and select **Forward**. Address the message, make changes as needed and click **Send**.

Sharing a feed sends the link to subscribe to the feed rather than a specific article, as Figure 9.31 shows. The recipient can copy and paste the link into the feed reader, just like you add a feed into Outlook.

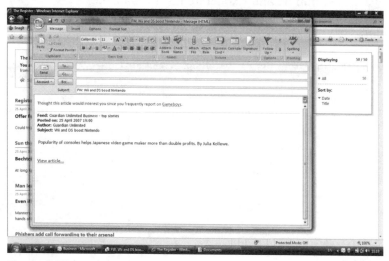

Figure 9.30

Forwarding an article from a feed in an e-mail message.

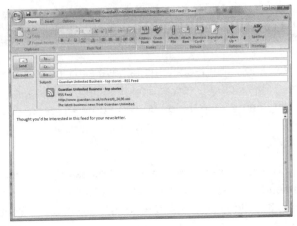

Figure 9.31

Sharing a feed in an e-mail message.

If you want to share multiple feeds, then exporting them as an
OPML may be the way to go. To export RSS Feeds to an OPML
file, do the following:

1 Select **Import and Export** from the File menu.

2 Select **Export RSS Feeds to an OPML file** and click **Next**.

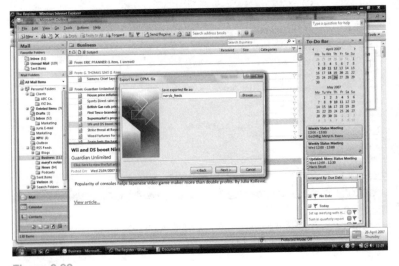

Figure 9.32

Saving an OPML file to the hard disk.

3 Check and uncheck the feeds you want to export. Use **Select All** and **Clear All**, if needed. Click **Next**.

4 Enter a name for the file, as Figure 9.32 shows, and click **Next**.

Outlook saves the file. You can e-mail the file as an attachment, as Figure 9.33 shows.

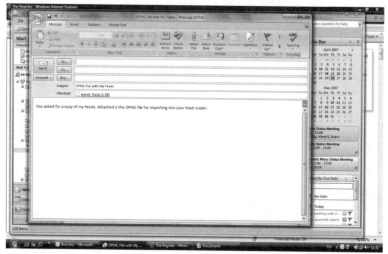

Figure 9.33
E-mailing the OPML file as an attachment.

10

Managing Menus, Toolbars and Data Files

In this lesson you'll discover how to use the Quick Access Toolbar, the Advanced Toolbar and how to personalise menus and toolbars.

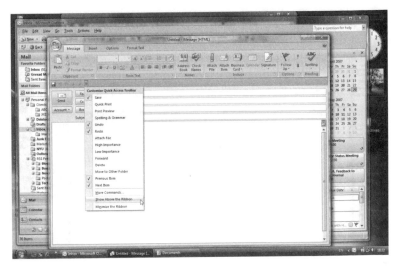

Figure 10.4
Accessing the Customize Quick Access Toolbar menu.

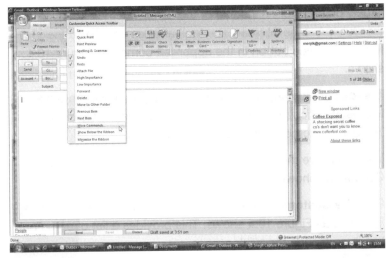

Figure 10.5
Accessing the Editor Options window to customise the Quick Access
Toolbar.

To view other commands, click **Popular Commands** for a list, as
Figure 10.6 shows.

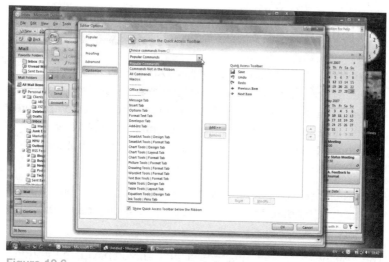

Figure 10.6
Viewing other commands.

The options on the left from Popular to Advanced contain the
default and current settings for Microsoft Office programs. Click
Advanced for a list of Outlook options, as Figure 10.7 shows.
Tweak them to your preferences.

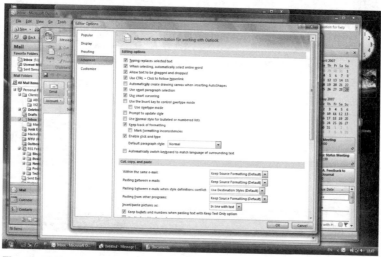

Figure 10.7
Viewing Outlook's advanced customisation options.

Outlook has three toolbars: Standard, Advanced and Web. Standard contains the basic e-mail tools, such as New, Reply to, Forward and Send/Receive. Outlook's Web toolbar also appears in Internet Explorer 6. The interface for Internet Explorer 7 rearranges the same buttons from the Web toolbar, but they appear on the browser's main menus.

The Advanced Toolbar resembles the Web Toolbar. Figure 10.8 shows the Standard toolbar followed by the Advanced and Web toolbars.

The Advanced Toolbar changes slightly as you navigate through the different modules. The following buttons appear in the Advanced Toolbar for all modules:

■ **Outlook Today**: Opens Outlook Today with an overview of your day's Calendar, Tasks and Messages, as shown in Figure 10.9.

Figure 10.8
Viewing the Standard, Advance and Web toolbars.

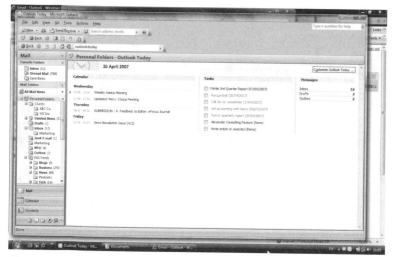

Figure 10.9
Viewing the overview of the day in Outlook Today.

- **Back, Forward and Up One Level**: Move around Outlook to the previous and next view page. Up One Level works only when you're not in a top-level folder.

- **Reading Pane**: Turn off the Reading Pane or view the bottom

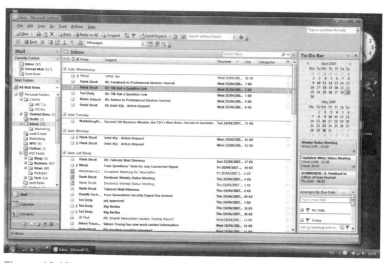

Figure 10.10
The Advanced Toolbar in the Mail console.

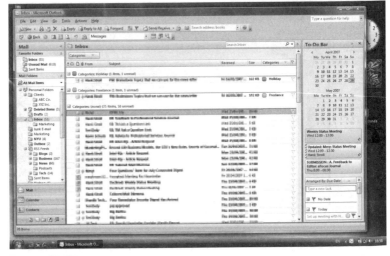

Figure 10.15
The Group By Box shows the current field used to sort the items.

The following buttons appear in one or more of the Advance Toolbars:

- **Rules and Alerts**: Opens the Rules and Alert window for automatically managing e-mail messages.

Figure 10.16
Sorting Contacts by Company name.

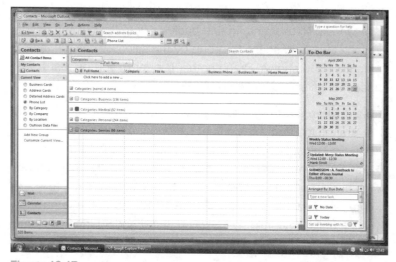

Figure 10.17
Using more than one field to sort Contacts.

■ **Current View**: Changes the current view to another view, as shown in Figures 10.13 and 10.14 for Calendar and Mail, respectively.

■ **Group By Box**: Shows which field the messages are sorted

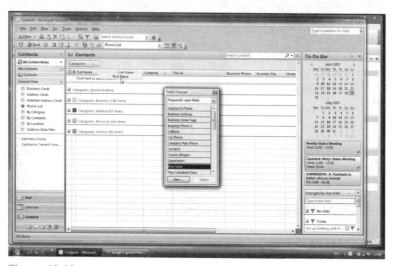

Figure 10.18
Adding First Name to Contact's content pane.

by, as Figure 10.15 shows. Click the box to switch from ascending to descending and back, or drag the column header to the indicated space to group by the selected column, as Figure 10.16 shows. Drag another header to sort by that field second, as shown in Figure 10.17.

- **Field Chooser**: drag fields to the content pane to add fields, or drag fields from the content pane to the Field Chooser to remove fields. Remove the field by selecting the field and dragging it into the Field Chooser window. Figure 10.18 shows the adding of the First Name field to the content pane to display contact first names. Figure 10.19 shows the removing of the Full Name field by selecting and dragging the Full Name field into the Field Chooser window.

- **AutoPreview**: Switches between one line message text to three lines of message text. AutoPreview won't show more than one line in Contacts unless there are notes included in the Contact's profile. Figure 10.20 shows the open profile and Figure 10.21 shows AutoPreview.

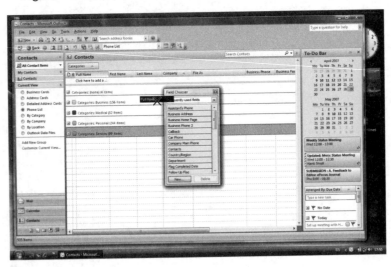

Figure 10.19

Removing Full Name from the headers in Contacts.

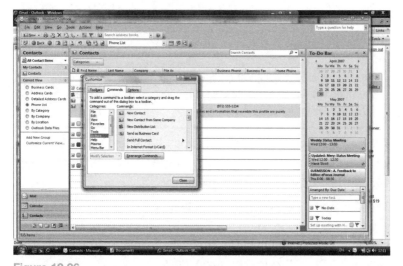

Figure 10.26
Selecting a command to add to a toolbar.

3 Select a category from the Categories column to find the command you want, as Figure 10.26 shows.

4 Drag the command from the Commands list to the toolbar where you want it to appear, as shown in Figure 10.27.

Figure 10.27
Adding a button to a toolbar.

Important

For as long as the Customize window is open, you won't be able to use Outlook's features. Having Customize open is akin to having Outlook in editor mode.

The new button appears in the toolbar. If the text is too long or you prefer an image, keep the Customize window open to make changes, as Figure 10.28 shows.

The new button appears in the toolbar. If the text is too long or you prefer an image, keep the Customize window open to make changes. Not all commands come with an image. You can change command in the following ways:

- Change the name by modifying the text in the Name box.

- Edit Button Image. If one doesn't exist, it's blank.

- Change Button Image by selecting an icon from a short list, as Figure 10.29 shows.

- Assign a hyperlink. This is not just for websites. The command can also link to files.

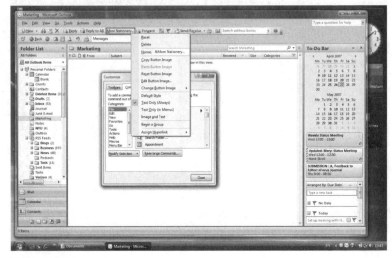

Figure 10.28
Modifying the button's appearance.

Figure 10.35

Viewing the the new toolbar.

5 Add buttons and commands in the toolbar as explained on page 200.

6 Continue adding buttons and commands until you have completed the toolbar. Figure 10.36 shows an example.

Figure 10.36

Creating and customising a toolbar.

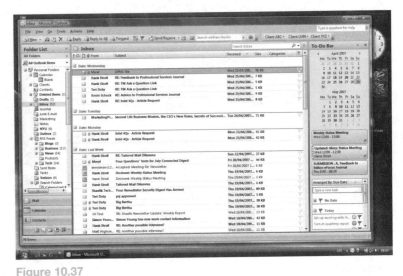

Figure 10.37

Moving and docking the new toolbar.

The new toolbar doesn't have to float in Outlook. Select and drag the toolbar above, below or next to the Standard toolbar, if you'd like it there, as Figure 10.37 shows.

Jargon buster

A **floating toolbar** is a toolbar that appears in front of Outlook's content and doesn't snap itself in place anywhere on the edge of Outlook's window. A **docked toolbar** snaps in place on the edge of Outlook's window, like the default Standard toolbar.

Open the Customize window from the Tools menu any time you want to add, change or remove items from the toolbar. Just as with removing a button, select the button or command to move and drag it to the Customize window.

You can also Rename and Delete a toolbar from the Customize window. Select the toolbar to rename or delete, and click **Rename** or **Delete**. Enter the new name in the Rename Toolbar

or confirm you wish to delete the toolbar in the delete toolbar
confirmation window, as Figures 10.38 and 10.39 show.

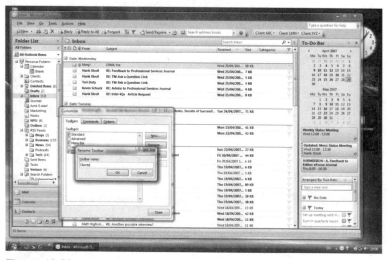

Figure 10.38
Renaming a toolbar.

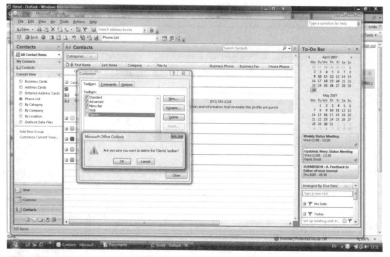

Figure 10.39
Deleting a toolbar.

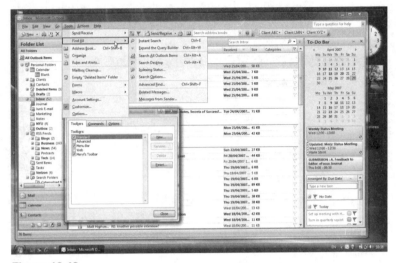

Figure 10.40

Viewing the original Find All menu from the Tools menu.

Important

You can't reset a custom toolbar.

Figure 10.41

Viewing the modified Find All menu.

Figure 10.42

Resetting the Find All menu to return to the original settings.

If you changed an item in a menu, you can reset the menu rather than the entire toolbar. For example, if you delete items from the Find All menu in the Tools menu and later you change your mind and want the items back, you can reset the menu. Figure 10.40 shows the original Find All menu.

Figure 10.41 shows a modified Find All menu with deleted items.

Use the following steps to restore the commands in the Find All or other similar menus with deleted items:

1. Click **Customize** from the Tools menu.

2. Click **Tools**.

3. Right-click **Find All** and select **Reset**, as Figure 10.42 shows.

4. Close the Customize window.

Changing the Size and Shape of Toolbars

The toolbars can move around Outlook, dock or float. You can also change the shape of a floating toolbar and change the size of a docked toolbar. Move any toolbar by selecting the move

Figure 10.43
Moving a docked toolbar to a new location.

handle (four dots on the far left side of a toolbar) and moving the toolbar to its new location as shown in Figure 10.43.

For docked toolbars, click on the Title Bar and drag it to a new spot, as Figure 10.44 shows.

Figure 10.44
Moving a floating toolbar to a new location.

Figure 10.45

Changing the size of a docked toolbar.

To change the shape of a floating toolbar, move the cursor over one of its edges at the top/bottom for taller or shorter or left/right for longer or narrower, until a two-directional arrow appears. Click and drag the edge, as Figure 10.45 shows.

Figure 10.46

Selecting the toolbar to change its size.

Figure 10.47
Viewing the changed sizes of the Standard and Web toolbars.

When resizing the docked toolbars, you can't change the size of a toolbar that appears on a row by itself. However, if you have two toolbars on the same row, you can resize them. Click the empty space of the toolbar you want to resize until you see a cursor with four arrows, as shown in Figure 10.46. Figure 10.47 shows a resized toolbar with the Standard toolbar showing fewer commands and the Web toolbar on the left showing more commands.

Changing Menu Behaviour

If you upgraded from Office 2003, you may continue to see only a part of a selected menu, which expands after a short delay or after selecting the arrows at the bottom of the menu. The settings from Outlook 2003 carry forward to Office 2007 upgrades. Office 2007 returns to full menus.

Do you prefer menus the 2003 way or the 2007 way? To switch between menu styles, select **Customize** from the Tools menu. Select the **Options** tab and check or uncheck the boxes based on your preference, as Figure 10.48 shows, along with the options for menu animations.

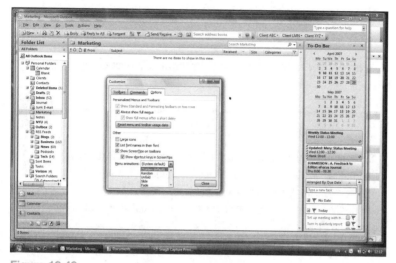

Figure 10.48

Customising options for menus and toolbars.

You can also do the following in the Options tab:

■ Change the icon size from large to small, and back.

■ Show font names using their style, as shown in Figure 10.49.

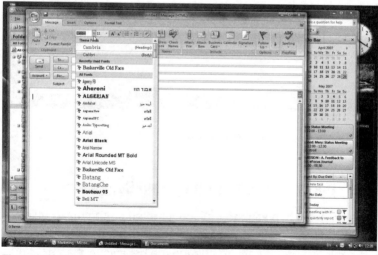

Figure 10.49

Viewing the font names in their style.

- Turn on and off ScreenTips.

- Turn on and off shortcut keys in ScreenTips.

- Modify how menu animation appears when opening a menu.

Jargon buster

ScreenTips, also referred to as tooltips, show a small text box when the mouse pointer hovers over an icon, command, button or other interface element. The text box displays the item's name or description. Figure 10.50 shows the ScreenTip and shortcut key for the printer icon.

Figure 10.50
Viewing the printer icon's ScreenTip.

Using Hyperlinks with Buttons and Commands

You can use a hyperlink to replace a button or command unless the item displays a menu or list when selected. To use a hyperlink, you don't have to change the behaviour of an existing button or command. Instead, create a new one and associate the hyperlink with it. For example, you can create a command for creating a new e-mail message with some of its information filled in. The following steps create a new command with a hyperlink that opens an already existing Outlook template:

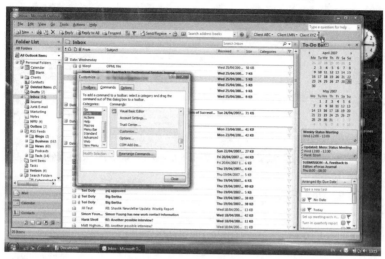

Figure 10.51
Adding a new button to a toolbar.

1. Select **Customize** from the Tools menu.

2. Select **Tools** from the Categories list, and scroll down to Customize.

3. Drag **Customize** to a toolbar, as Figure 10.51 shows.

4. Right-click **Customize** with the Customize window still open, and enter a new name in the Name box, as Figure 10.52 shows.

5. Right-click **Customize** again, and select **Assign Hyperlink** and **Open**, as Figure 10.53 shows.

6. Browse to Office Templates, which is typically located at *C:\Users\[user name]\AppData\Local\Microsoft\Templates*.

7. Select the template to associate with the command, as Figure 10.54 shows, and click **OK**.

Figure 10.52
Giving a name to the new button.

8 Click **Close** on the Customize window.

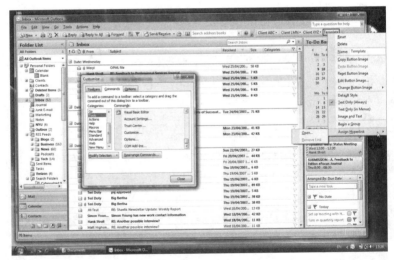

Figure 10.53
Opening the Assign Hyperlink window.

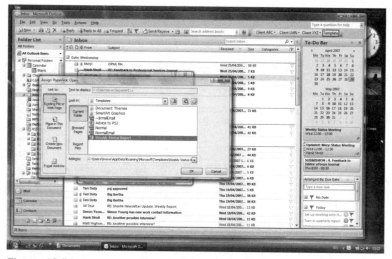

Figure 10.54

Assigning a template to a hyperlink.

Click **Template** or whatever you named the new button. You may get a Microsoft Office Outlook Security Notice. If so, click **Yes** and **Open**. The new e-mail message appears along with any content included in the template, as Figure 10.55 shows. Hyperlinks can also link to websites and documents.

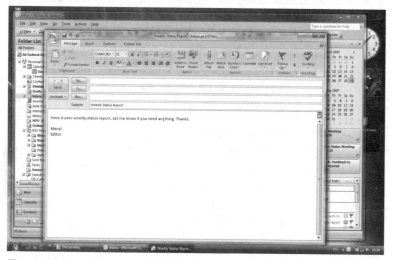

Figure 10.55

Opening the template associated with the Status Report button.

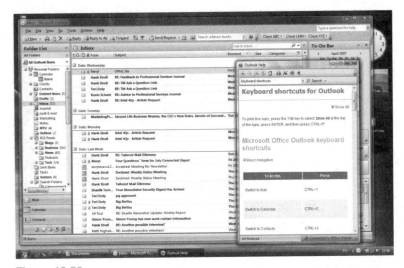

Figure 10.56
Viewing the list of keyboard shortcuts from Outlook Help.

→ Using Keyboard Shortcuts and Keyboard Accessible

Many users rely on **Ctrl+C** and **Ctrl+V** for copy and paste, since it's faster than selecting the menu and then the command. You can see a list of keyboard shortcuts in the Help file by selecting **Accessibility** and **Keyboard shortcuts for Outlook**, or do a search for **keyboard shortcuts**, as Figure 10.56 shows.

You can access commands that have an underline beneath a letter by pressing **Alt+[underlined letter]**. Open menus show the keyboard shortcuts next to the commands. Also from within an open menu, you can press the down and up arrow keys to move around the menu. Use the right arrow key to navigate over to a menu with a submenu as identified with an arrow pointing right, such as Follow Up under Actions. With **Follow Up** selected, press the right arrow key to see its submenu, as Figure 10.57 shows.

Figure 10.57

Using the keyboard to navigate the menu and submenu.

Users can use the keyboard instead of the mouse to accomplish tasks tagged with keyboard accessible.

11

Managing Data and More E-mail Topics

In this lesson you'll learn about data files, backing up, archiving and restoring data.

Outlook saves data in a personal folder file, which uses the .pst extension. A typical PST file contains data from Calendar, Mail, Contacts, Tasks and your personal folders. Users on an Exchange Server have data stored in an Exchange Server mailbox that lives on a server instead of the local computer. The only way to access this data store is by connecting to the server.

Outlook also creates an Offline Folder File with an .ost extension. This stores your data for working when your computer isn't connected to the Internet or network. If the server is down or you are away from the office and its network, the Exchange Server data file continues to receive messages and manage files as it always does. You can create e-mail messages and new folders and file e-mail messages into folders while offline. Any work done offline goes into the OST file, which synchronises with the Exchange Server the next time it connects.

Jargon buster

Outlook 2007 relies on **Cached Exchange Mode**, which provides a copy of your mailbox on your computer and synchronises with the Exchange Server. Cached Exchange Mode always uses an OST file, regardless of whether a connection is active. The great thing about this feature is that you can lose a connection to the server and continue working in Outlook as if nothing has happened.

It's possible to have a PST file even with an Exchange Server account. However, any changes to the PST file don't synchronise with Exchange.

Timesaver tip

Working with at least two computers is common today. If you want your second computer to have the same Outlook folders and data as on your main computer, just copy the PST file to your second computer. In Outlook, open **Account Settings** from the Tool menu and select the **Data Files** tab. Click **Add**, leave the Types of storage selection as is, and click **OK** to locate the PST file. Select the file and click **OK**. Give it a name in the Create Microsoft Personal Folders window, as Figure 11.1 shows, and click **OK**. Close Account Settings, and the new personal folders file appears in the Navigation Pane, as Figure 11.2 shows. You can also import a PST file using Import and Export from the File menu.

Figure 11.1

Creating a new personal folders file.

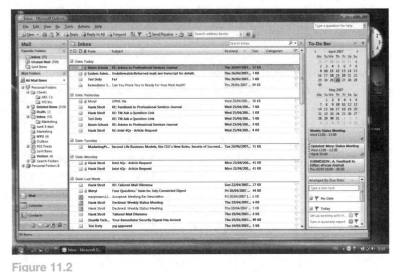

Figure 11.2

The new personal folders file appears in the Navigation Pane.

→ Backing up and Restoring Data

The stories of crashed computers, dead hard drives and lost files never end. Computers may not have a human heart, but they run into plenty of health challenges to threaten your data. No matter how well you take care of your computer, its hard drive can crash and take your valuable data with it. The operating system can go berserk, creating corrupted files. Spyware, viruses and nasties can also do quirky things to your computer. Backing up your data is one of the most important activities in managing your computer.

Backing up your PST file saves you lots of time should you ever run into the need for a copy. Better still, save a copy of your PST file on a server or network drive that runs independently of your computer. Saving a backup file to the same computer loaded with Outlook won't help in many cases. If your hard drive crashes, for example, it affects both Outlook and the backup file. The following steps walk you through backing up Outlook data.

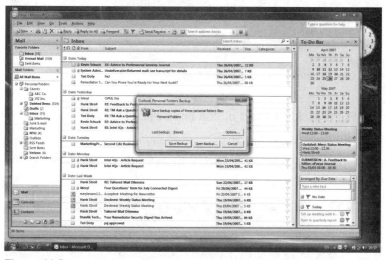

Figure 11.3

Using the Microsoft Outlook Personal Folder Backup tool to automatically back up Outlook's data files.

You don't have to use a backup tool to save your data. Instead, you can copy the PST file and save it elsewhere. To find out the location of your PST file, do the following:

1. Go to **Account Settings** in the Tools menu.

2. Select the **Data Files** tab and double-click the **Personal Folder** you wish to back up.

3. Put your cursor into the **Filename** box, click the box twice to highlight the line and press **Ctrl+C** to copy it.

Figure 11.4

Opening Explorer to find the PST files.

4 Right-click the **Start** button and select **Explore**.

5 Put your cursor into the folder location box, as shown in Figure 11.4 and press **Ctrl+V** to paste the location of the personal folders file.

Figure 11.5

Finding the location of the PST files.

6 Delete the PST file name (Outlook.pst, for example) and press **Enter** to find the PST file, as Figure 11.5 shows.

7 Save the file to a network drive or online storage website.

To restore the data, do the following:

1 Locate the backup copy of the PST file. Right-click the file and choose **Copy**.

2 Right-click **Start** and select **Explore**.

3 Find the folder where the original PST file lives (default *C:\Users\[your user name]\AppData\Local\Microsoft\Outlook\ Outlook.pst*) and press **Ctrl+V** to paste the file.

4 Open Outlook to confirm the data appears.

→ Archiving Data   11

Although it's nice to have e-mail messages available for when you need them, having too many affects your computer's performance. Professional life organisers recommend giving away possessions you haven't used in over a year. Similarly, you can archive items that you haven't opened in a year or two. You can always get them later if you need them again. Rather than having to do the cleaning, let AutoArchive do the dirty work.

Use AutoArchive to automatically move important but infrequently used items to an archive file and to permanently delete expired items. The following is the default location and name for the archive file: *C:\Documents and Settings\[your user name]\Local Settings\Application Data\Microsoft\Outlook\ Archive.pst*.

Archived items appear in the Archives Folder in the Outlook Folder List located in the Navigation Pane, as Figure 11.6 shows.

Figure 11.6

Archived items go into the Archive folders.

You may want to back up the archive file in the same way as you back up the PST file. Recovering a PST file alone won't recover your archived file. Consider backing up both files at the same time.

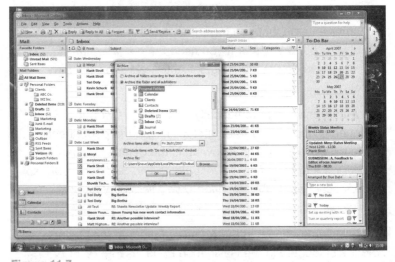

Figure 11.7

Manually archiving Outlook items.

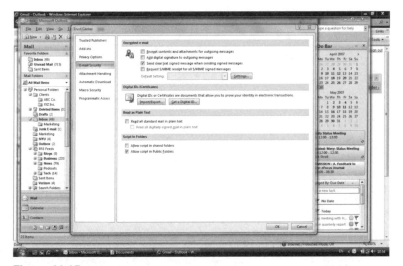

Figure 11.15
Managing e-mail security options.

One approach is to use a digital signature, which relies on code
to prove the message comes from a valid associated e-mail
account and computer. Sign all outgoing messages with a digital
signature using the following steps:

1 Select **Trust Center** from the Tools menu.

2 Select **E-mail Security** from the Trust Center Navigation
Pane, as shown in Figure 11.15.

3 Check the box next to Add digital signature to outgoing
messages.

4 Check the box next to Send clear text signed message when
sending signed messages, and click **OK**.

Jargon buster

Secure Multipurpose Internet Mail Extensions (S/MIME) is a public
key encryption standard for digitally signing and authenticating e-mail
messages.

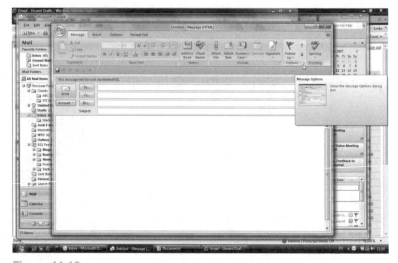

Figure 11.16
Opening Message Options.

When you want to digital sign an e-mail message, select the **Digital Signature** icon in the Options group on the Message tab. This may not appear the first time you try to use the feature or if you don't yet have a Digital ID. Instead, click the square icon next to Options to open the Message Options window, as Figure 11.16 shows.

Do the following in the Message Options window to send the current message with a digital signature:

1 Click **Security Settings**.

2 Click the checkbox next to Add digital signature to this message, as shown in Figure 11.17, and click **OK**.

3 Close the Message Options window.

Encryption provides another option for securing e-mail, but reading it requires the recipient's e-mail application to have a private key matching the public key that the sender used to encrypt the message. Encryption scrambles the text of an e-mail message and then unscrambles it if the recipient has a

> **Important**
>
> If you attach a message that isn't rights-managed to a rights-managed e-mail message, the attached file isn't rights-managed because IRM doesn't work with MSG files.

To use IRM requires access to an IRM server. If you're on an Exchange Server, ask your system administrator about IRM. Microsoft provides an IRM server and offers a free trial of the service.

A simple thing to do that boosts your e-mail security is to receive e-mail messages in plain text. Viruses and bad ware not only spread through opening attached files; they can also spread through the code behind the HTML. Plain text means no colour, no bold, no large and small font sizes, no images appearing in the body of the message. Sounds dull, but it protects you and your computer. Your e-mail messages will load faster as an added bonus. Change your options for receiving incoming e-mail messages as plain text by opening the Trust Center from the Tools menu. Select **E-mail Security** from the left pane. Under the Read as Plain Text section, check the box next to Read all standard mail in plain text. Click **OK** and your e-mail messages will appear in plain text.

→ Managing Junk E-mail

The Junk E-mail Filter aims to send spam and other unwanted e-mail messages to your Junk folder. Outlook turns on the filter by default with the protection level set to Low. To view Junk E-mail Options, select **Junk E-mail** from the Actions menu and click **Junk E-mail Options**, as shown in Figure 11.19.

The filter also reviews all incoming messages for phishing, so you don't submit personal information to a fraudulent website that resembles a real website. The Options page, by default, disables links and scripts in phishing messages.

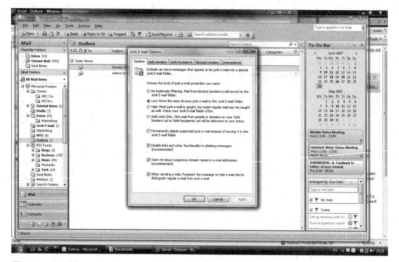

Figure 11.19

Viewing the Junk-E-mail Options window.

You can change the level of filtering protection to the following:

■ **No Automatic Filtering**: Outlook won't filter any messages
unless they're from senders on your Blocked Senders list, as
Figure 11.20 shows.

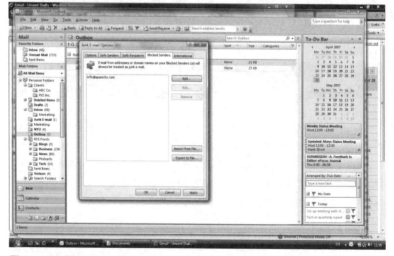

Figure 11.20

Managing the Blocked Senders list.

Figure 11.21
Managing the Safe Senders list.

■ **Low**: Less likely to move non-junk messages into the junk folder, but more junk messages will appear in the inbox than they do on High setting.

■ **High**: More likely to catch all junk messages, but could have

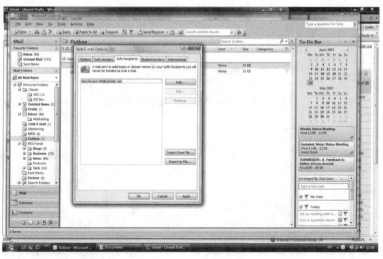

Figure 11.22
Adding, editing and removing items from the Safe Recipients list.

false positives and send legitimate messages into the junk folder.

■ **Safe Lists Only**: The only messages you receive in your inbox are those e-mail addresses and domains like *companyname.com* listed in your Safe Senders and Safe Recipient lists, as Figures 11.21 and 11.22 show.

Add, edit and remove e-mail addresses and domain names in the Safe Senders, Safe Recipients and Blocked Senders tabs using the **Add, Edit** and **Remove** buttons in each tab. Some websites publish text files with known addresses that you can import into the Blocked Senders list. However, spammers never stick with an address for long, and it's impossible to keep up with all the bad senders out there on the Internet.

You can share your lists with family members, colleagues and other computers by clicking **Export to File**. Enter a file name and click **Save**, as Figure 11.23 shows.

Modify the last four options on the Options tab to your preferences. The International tab lets you filter e-mail messages

Figure 11.23

Exporting the Safe Senders list to share with others.

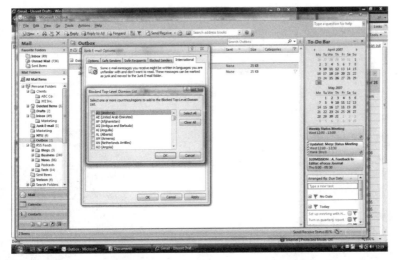

Figure 11.24

Selecting top-level domains to block e-mail messages from those domains.

appearing in languages other than your own to the Junk folder. If you don't have family, friends or colleagues in countries using top-level domains such as AD (Andorra) and ZW (Zimbabwe), you may want to block messages from those top-level domains, as Figure 11.24 shows.

You can do the same for encodings, which blocks e-mail messages appearing in selected languages, as Figure 11.25 shows.

The Junk E-mail Filter deems all e-mail addresses in Contacts as safe. However, you may have e-mail addresses that are not in Contacts but that you wish to add to the Safe Senders list. Click the **Safe Senders** tab on the Junk E-mail Options window and click **Add**. Enter the relevant e-mail addresses or top-level domains and click **OK**.

These steps also work for the other Junk E-mail Options window tabs. Also on the Safe Senders tab, you can check or uncheck the boxes for trusting e-mails from your contacts and automatically adding e-mail addresses of people you send e-mails to on the Safe Senders list.

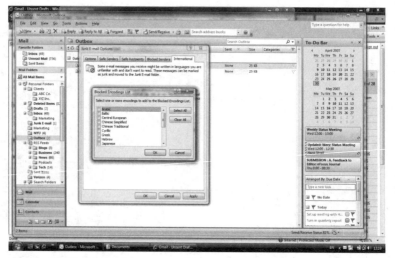

Figure 11.25

Selecting encodings to block e-mail messages appearing in selected languages.

No matter what steps you take to filter the junk, no filtering process is perfect. On occasion, you might want to check your Junk folder to ensure no legitimate e-mails appear in the folder. If they do, move them to the inbox and add the e-mail address to the Safe Senders list.

If you're not sure about an e-mail that asks for your personal information, go to your Internet browser and enter the website's URL instead of clicking the link from within the e-mail message. If a legitimate website needs information from you, it will let you know on its website. Stay safe.